THE MACM

Greek Gods and Heroes

Editorial review, Foreword, and Afterword by

BARRY R. KATZ, Ph.D.

Adjunct Assistant Professor of Classics

New York University

THE MACMILLAN BOOK OF

Greek Gods and Heroes

BY ALICE LOW

Illustrated by Arvis Stewart

ALADDIN BOOKS

Macmillan Publishing Company
NEW YORK

Maxwell Macmillan Canada
TORONTO

Maxwell Macmillan International
NEW YORK   OXFORD   SINGAPORE   SYDNEY

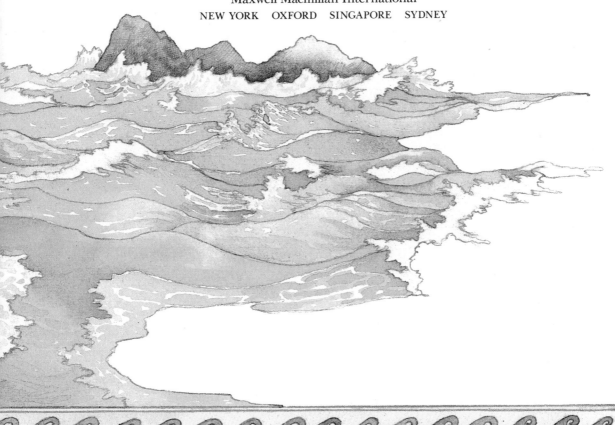

To Andy, Kathy, Margie, Laurent,
Victoria, and Stephanie

A.L.

For Mary

A.S.

First Aladdin Books edition 1994
Copyright © 1985 by Macmillan Publishing Company, a division of
Macmillan, Inc.

Aladdin Books
Macmillan Publishing Company
866 Third Avenue
New York, NY 10022

Maxwell Macmillan Canada, Inc.
1200 Eglinton Avenue East
Suite 200
Don Mills, Ontario M3C 3N1

Macmillan Publishing Company is part of the Maxwell Communication
Group of Companies.
Printed in the United States of America
10 9 8 7 6 5 4 3 2 1

Library of Congress Cataloging-in-Publication Data
Low, Alice.
The Macmillan book of Greek gods and heroes /
by Alice Low ; illustrated by Arvis Stewart.
— 1st Aladdin Books ed.
p.   cm.
Originally published: New York : Macmillan ; London :
Collier Macmillan, ©1985.
Includes index.
Summary: Recreates the popular myths of ancient Greece,
including the legand of Odysseus.
ISBN 0-689-71874-8
1. Mythology, Greek—Juvenile literature. [1. Mythology,
Greek.] I. Stewart, Arvis L., ill. II. Title. III. Title:
Greek gods and heroes.
[BL782.L68   1994]
292.1′3—dc20   94-3198

Contents

Foreword vii

❧ Contents ❧

Foreword

~~~~~~~~~~

The best stories anyone has ever heard, with the most interesting characters imaginable—that is what this book contains. The myths of the ancient Greeks have always been fascinating. Happily, though, they are even more.

These stories tell us what the people of ancient Greece thought about their world. They believed there were many gods and that those gods controlled the universe. For example, Zeus, the greatest god, was in charge of the weather, of thunder and lightning. When it thundered, the ancient Greeks thought Zeus was at work. An ancient weatherman, cloud-gathering Zeus did not predict the weather: He *made* it!

What is more, the ancient Greeks believed that all of nature—trees and mountains and rivers and rocks—either was or contained gods and goddesses. Many stories explained nature. If the pattern of particular stars in the sky looked like a bull, people told a story about a bull that had been placed in the sky long before. The natural world, then, was alive: It had feelings; it had to be treated with respect.

The ancient Greeks also believed that the gods and goddesses were not very different from human beings. They were just another family. Zeus was the father, his wife, Hera, was the mother, and there were various children and relatives. Zeus and Hera loved each other, but sometimes they argued and even fought. Zeus thought *he* was the head of the family, but occasionally Hera outsmarted him.

Mount Olympus, home of the gods, seems to us an ancient theater where drama was performed by a large cast of characters. The Greeks, though, believed that these characters really existed and influenced human lives. Often, the myths tell us, the gods even married human beings and became the fathers and mothers of humans.

Gods and humans—what was the basic difference between them? Was it strength? Most gods and goddesses were stronger than humans, but a few humans, great heroes like Heracles, were stronger than many gods. Intelligence was not the difference, either. Ares, the god of war, was very stupid. No, the basic difference between humans and gods was mortality, death. Humans died; gods never died. Humans were temporary, but gods were permanent. Of all the human heroes, only Heracles was allowed to join the gods on Olympus, as husband of Hebe, goddess of youth. Heracles was made young again and given immortality.

These myths were shaped by history and society. The ancient Greeks were a mixture of two peoples, one who worshipped male sky gods, like Zeus, and another who worshipped earth goddesses. Because the two peoples fought and the sky-god worshippers conquered the others, Zeus and his brothers became the rulers of the divine world. Zeus and other gods were believed to be fathers of various mortals because many aristocrats liked to claim that they were children of gods.

In other words, these stories about Olympian deities reflect the human world of ancient Greece—its understanding of nature, its personal relationships, and its wars. They tell us much about ancient Greece, and they give us much pleasure.

THE MACMILLAN BOOK OF

Greek Gods and Heroes

Mother Earth
and Her Children

⌇⌇⌇⌇⌇⌇⌇⌇⌇⌇⌇⌇⌇⌇⌇⌇⌇⌇⌇⌇⌇⌇⌇⌇⌇⌇⌇⌇⌇⌇⌇⌇

IN the very beginning, there was no earth or sea or sky. There was only a mass of confusion in darkness, called Chaos.

After many, many years, Mother Earth, named Gaea, was born out of Chaos. And after many more years, she gave birth to a son, Uranus, who was Father Heaven.

Father Heaven loved Mother Earth, and he made rain fall on her, so that flowers and trees and grass grew. The rain also fell into hollows and crevices, forming seas and rivers and lakes. Then Mother Earth created many kinds of animals to live in the forests and fields and oceans and lakes.

Mother Earth and Father Heaven had many children. First Mother Earth gave birth to three monstrous sons, each with fifty heads and one hundred hands. Then she gave birth to three more gigantic sons, just as ugly, called the Cyclopes. Each Cyclops had only one eye right in the middle of his forehead. These six sons were as strong as earthquakes and tornados put together. And they were often as destructive.

Finally Mother Earth bore the first gods, six sons and six daughters called the Titans. They, too, were gigantic, yet somewhat more like humans than her first children. They were just as strong as her first six sons, but sometimes they used their power wisely.

Father Heaven could not stand the sight of his first six ugly sons, and he was afraid of them, too. One day he threw them into a dark hole under the earth.

Mother Earth cried bitterly over this cruelty to her children. She decided to destroy Father Heaven and bring back her beloved children. She made a weapon, a sickle, and gave it to the Titans. "Kill your cruel father," she begged them, "and then go down into that dark hole and bring your brothers back to me."

Cronus, the strongest and bravest of the Titans, led the attack on his father and wounded him dreadfully. Then he released his brothers. The Titans made Cronus the ruler of heaven and earth and their sister, Rhea, his wife and queen.

But power changed Cronus, and now *he* imprisoned his brothers, the one-eyed Cyclopes and the hundred-handed monsters, in that dark hole under the earth.

This enraged Mother Earth, but she did not tell Cronus how she felt. She bided her time while Cronus's wife, Rhea, bore sons, for she knew that one of them was destined to overthrow Cronus.

Cronus, too, knew that one of his children was to rise up

against him and take his place as king of the gods. Therefore, to keep his children from growing up and becoming powerful, he swallowed them as soon as they were born.

Rhea was deeply saddened as, one by one, Cronus devoured her first five children: Hestia, Demeter, Hera, Hades, and Poseidon. When she was expecting her sixth child, she determined to save it from Cronus. After her baby son, Zeus, was born, she gave him to Mother Earth, who hid the baby in a cave on the island of Crete.

Then Rhea went to Cronus and said, "Here is our sixth child, a son. Do whatever you wish with him." She handed Cronus a bundle that looked like a baby wrapped in a blanket.

Of course Cronus swallowed it, just as Rhea had expected.

But Cronus had swallowed a stone wrapped in a blanket, not the baby Zeus.

Now Rhea was happy. She hoped that Zeus was the son who would destroy his frightful father, Cronus.

*

Zeus grew up on Crete among shepherds and nymphs, far from his wicked father, Cronus. He drank the milk of a goat nymph, who fed him honey, too. He slept in a golden cradle that was hung from a tree, and armed guards protected him. Whenever he cried, the guards banged their spears on their shields so that Cronus would not hear Zeus's loud wails and know that he still lived.

Nevertheless Cronus learned that his son was alive on Crete, and he went after him, intending to swallow him. But Zeus was too clever for Cronus. He changed himself into a serpent, and though Cronus searched high and low, he could not find Zeus.

Rhea, Zeus's mother, had told him about the terrible deeds

of his father, and Zeus vowed that when he was fully grown, he would rescue his brothers and sisters.

At last that time came. Zeus returned to Rhea and disguised himself as a servant in Cronus's palace. Then he and Rhea laid their plot. "If you will concoct a poisonous potion," said Zeus to his mother, "I will mix it into Cronus's drink." His mother agreed readily, and when the poisoned drink had been prepared, Zeus served it to Cronus. Cronus drank it quickly, for he was thirsty. He became very ill and vomited up the stone he had swallowed. The pains continued as, one by one, out of Cronus's mouth sprang his five children.

Zeus's brothers and sisters hugged him and thanked him for giving them new life. "And now that you have set us free," they said to Zeus, "you must lead us in a battle against Cronus and the Titans. We, not they, must rule the universe, and never again will we be imprisoned."

*

The terrible war raged for ten long years. Cronus was no longer young, so Atlas led the Titans. However, two other Titans, Prometheus and Epimetheus, joined Zeus and his brothers and sisters. That made the two sides nearly equal in strength. Neither could win.

Finally wise Mother Earth told Zeus that his side would be victorious if he followed her advice. "Go down into the dark hole under the earth and release the one-eyed Cyclopes and their hundred-handed brothers, for they shall help you win."

Zeus followed Mother Earth's advice and descended bravely into the dark hole. He killed the guard and freed the prisoners. Then he gave them divine food and drink, and at last their strength returned.

The Cyclopes, in turn, gave Zeus gifts to use as weapons against Cronus and the Titans.

"To Zeus," said one of the Cyclopes, "we give our powerful weapons, the thunderbolts."

"To Zeus's brother Hades," said another, "we give this magic helmet of darkness."

"And to their brother Poseidon," said the third, "we give this sharp-pronged trident."

Zeus and Hades and Poseidon thanked the Cyclopes and discussed how best to use their gifts.

Then Hades put on his helmet of darkness, which made him invisible. He crept up behind Cronus and stole his weapons.

Poseidon struck the ground with his trident, which caused the earth to shake. Cronus, terrified, became powerless.

Then Zeus threw his thunderbolts, and Cronus and Atlas and the rest of the Titans retreated.

Meanwhile the three hundred-handed brothers hurled three hundred rocks at the Titans, all at once, over and over.

The earth was almost torn apart by the dreadful battle, but before it could be destroyed, Zeus and his brothers and sisters won. They punished all the Titans except for Prometheus and Epimetheus, who had helped them. They made Atlas, the Titans' leader, carry the whole sky on his shoulders, forever. And they chained Cronus and the others in the dark hole under the earth.

Zeus could not rest long, though, for Mother Earth gave birth to one more enemy, the most terrible of all, a monster named Typhon. Typhon had one hundred heads and spurted a stream of fire from each eye. But Zeus hurled his thunderbolts and struck down that hideous creature. At last there was peace on earth.

Now, which of the three brothers, Zeus, Poseidon, or Hades, should be the ruler of the universe? They had had enough fighting, and they wanted to settle this problem without an argument.

They decided to draw lots. Hades won the underworld, and Poseidon won the sea. And Zeus became lord of heaven and ruler of all the gods of Mount Olympus.

The Gods and Goddesses
of Mount Olympus

THE summit of Mount Olympus, the highest mountain in Greece, was the home of most of the Greek gods and goddesses. They lived in a palace that was always filled with brilliant sunlight, for it never rained or snowed in that shining place.

The gods and goddesses of Olympus were immortal, which means that they could not die. No mortals were ever allowed to come to Mount Olympus, but the Olympians often visited earth by passing through a gate of clouds tended by four goddesses called the Seasons.

The chief god on Olympus was *Zeus*, lord of the sky, god of thunder and lightning, king of the gods. He was conceited and awesome but seldom frightening. Often he summoned the most important gods and goddesses to a meeting in the great hall of the palace. Their thrones were of gold and silver and marble and ivory, ornamented with precious stones. But the throne of Zeus was the largest and most magnificent of all.

11

Almost all of the gods and goddesses were Zeus's family, and each had special powers. Queen *Hera*, Zeus's beautiful wife and sister, was the goddess of marriage and protector of women. At first Hera had refused to become Zeus's wife. But he had caused a great thunderstorm and changed himself into a frightened bird. Hera had taken pity on him and hugged him tight. In that way he had won her, and in similar ways he continued to win other women, making Hera jealous and angry.

Zeus's stormy brother *Poseidon*, god of the sea, sometimes lived in a spendid palace beneath the ocean. Often he struck the sea with his trident, which was a fisherman's spear, stirring up wild tempests with howling winds and towering waves. But at other times he drove his golden chariot over the waves to quiet them. When he struck the ground, the earth quaked and split open. He gave people the first horse, which he claimed to have created. His wife was Amphitrite, a sea nymph, who bore him a son named Triton. Triton had a fishtail, and he rode a sea monster and blew a conch shell like a trumpet.

Zeus's other brother, *Hades*, did not live on Olympus. He was god of the underworld and the dead, and he rarely left his gloomy palace in his dark land. He was god of wealth, too, and very rich he was, for he owned all the precious metals under the earth.

Demeter was Zeus's sister and goddess of the harvest. It was she who made earth's fruits and grains grow and flourish. If not for Demeter, the earth would have been dry and barren, and people would have starved. Her daughter, Persephone, had been carried off to the underworld by Hades to be his queen. Demeter was happy only when Persephone came back to visit her each year.

Zeus's third sister was kind *Hestia*, goddess of the hearth and home. Her only job on Mount Olympus was keeping the fire lit in the palace hearth.

Zeus had eight sons and daughters on Olympus. All but *Hebe*, goddess of eternal youth and cupbearer to the gods, had thrones and took part in the meetings of the gods.

The twins *Apollo* and *Artemis* were his children by a Titan named Leto. She had given birth to them on the island of Delos, where Hera had chased her in a fit of jealousy.

Apollo, god of light and music and poetry, was the most beautiful of the gods. He was also the god of medicine and first taught people the art of healing. He was a fine marksman, too, and shot silver arrows from his silver bow. And at Delphi, on Mount Parnassus, he had an oracle through which he predicted the future. People came from far and wide to consult the oracle and find out the will of the gods.

Artemis, Apollo's twin sister, was goddess of hunting and of unmarried girls. She had decided never to marry. She spent her time roaming through the woods of earth with her nymphs and hounds, hunting with a silver bow. Sometimes she would bathe naked by moonlight in mountain pools. Once, when a mortal man saw her bathing, she threw a few drops of water on him, changing him into a stag. Then she had him killed by his own pack of dogs. Though she was often fierce, she had her tender side, too, and took care of mothers and their little children.

Zeus's favorite daughter was *Athena*, goddess of wisdom. She had sprung from his head fully grown and fully armed, wearing a shining helmet and a glimmering robe. Zeus's son Hephaestus had split open his father's head with an axe so that Athena could leap out. Athena was also the goddess of arts and crafts, skilled at pottery and weaving. And she was the protector of heroes in battle, leading armies whenever their causes were just. She watched over the city of Athens, as well. She had won that city in a contest with Poseidon when she gave its people her gift, the olive tree, a much more useful gift than Poseidon's spring of salty water.

Zeus and Hera's son *Hephaestus* was god of fire. He was the only ugly god, but he was peace loving and popular. He walked

with a limp because Zeus had thrown him over the palace walls one day when he had sided with his mother, Hera, in an argument. It had taken a whole day for him to fall from Olympus to earth, and he had landed with a terrible thump. Fortunately a sea goddess had found and nursed him until he could return to Olympus. He was a skilled craftsman and made all the Olympians' thrones, furniture, armor, and weapons. His own throne was a masterpiece. He had fashioned it to roll about under its own power! And he had invented and made three gold helpers who assisted him in his workshop. Hephaestus was also god of craftsmen and protector of blacksmiths, goldsmiths, and carpenters, among others. His wife was the radiant *Aphrodite*, goddess of love and beauty.

Even though she was not a child of Zeus, Aphrodite was an important goddess. She was lighthearted and full of laughter. Wherever she walked, flowers sprang up beneath her feet. Without her there would have been no beauty or joy. Nobody knew who her mother and father were. She had risen out of the foam of the sea, a lovely vision. The wind had carried her to the island of Cyprus on a conch shell. There the gods, sent by Zeus, had clothed her in shining robes and brought her to Olympus. Hephaestus had made her a magic belt, and when she wore it, men and gods fell wildly in love with her. Aphrodite had a son named Eros, whose father was the god Ares. Eros shot his arrows at mortals and gods and made them fall in love instantly.

Hermes was Zeus's graceful, happy son by a minor goddess named Maia. He was god of shepherds, merchants, and travelers—and thieves, too. He was a mischievous rascal. The day he was born he stole Apollo's herd of cows. Apollo forgave him when Hermes gave him the lyre, a small harp, which he had invented and made out of a tortoise shell. Hermes was also Zeus's messenger, for he could fly swiftly, wearing his winged sandals and winged cap. He had a more solemn duty, as well, that of guiding the souls of the dead to the underworld. Hermes had a son named Pan, who, like his father, was god of shepherds. He was also guardian of flocks and fields. Pan's mother was a wood nymph, and he was part goat, with horns and hoofs. He loved to dance with the nymphs and play sweet music on his pipes of reed, which he had invented.

Handsome *Ares*, god of war, was the son of Zeus and Hera. He was boastful and cruel and had no manners. He loved fighting, though he was a terrible coward when he was wounded. Eris, his sister, and her son, Strife, walked beside him and caused no end of conflict. Behind Ares walked Terror, Trembling, and Panic. Wherever he went, there was violence and bloodshed. He was the curse of mortals.

Dionysus, god of wine, was Zeus's youngest son. His mother, Semele, was a princess and a mortal woman. When Semele was with child, she did not know that Zeus was the father, because he had come to her in disguise. Out of jealousy, Hera told Semele the truth and persuaded her to ask Zeus to appear to her as god of thunder and lightning. Semele did so, and Zeus could not refuse to grant her this favor. But as soon as Semele beheld Zeus as a radiant god, she was consumed by fire.

The child, however, was saved by Hermes, who sewed him inside Zeus's leg. Soon he was born from there, a healthy god, Dionysus.

Hermes hid Dionysus from Hera in a valley. There, tended by nymphs, he grew strong, and he played happily with leopards and tigers. Some years later, Dionysus taught himself to make wine from the grapes that grew in the valley, and he traveled widely, teaching people the art of wine making.

Sometimes the gods and goddesses of Olympus quarreled so intensely that Zeus would threaten to throw a thunderbolt to quiet them. But most of the time they lived in peace and joy. They listened to Apollo's soft music, ate a delicious food called ambrosia, and drank nectar, which was served to them by Hebe. And when the immortal Olympians visited earth, they took an active part in the lives of mortal men and women.

Zeus and the Creation of Mankind

Prometheus and His Gift to Man

W HEN it was time for man to be created, Zeus gave this important work to Prometheus and Epimetheus, the two Titans who had helped him in his battle against Cronus and the other Titans. Zeus also assigned them the task of giving men and animals gifts that would insure their survival.

Prometheus, whose name means "forethought," was an inventor and exceedingly wise. His brother, Epimetheus, whose name means "afterthought," was just the opposite, exceedingly rash.

Epimetheus decided that *he* would give the gifts to the animals, and Prometheus set about creating the first man. He wanted man to be nobler than the animals, and he sat by the ocean for a long time, thinking. Finally he took a handful of

earth and added water to it, so that it would hold together when he shaped it. Then, slowly and carefully, he modeled the first man in the image of the gods. Prometheus gave him two feet on which to stand, so that he could look up to heaven and the stars, not down at the earth as the animals did.

Meanwhile Epimetheus was handing out gifts to the animals, which, until that time, had had no means of defense and looked very different from the way they do today. Epimetheus gave claws to the tigers, wings to the birds, and horns to the cattle. And then he gave some of the animals swiftness, others cunning and courage, and still others strength. He even gave many of them fur to keep them warm in winter.

Epimetheus was very pleased with himself. But then Prometheus ran up to him, shouting, "Look, brother. My man has come to life. Is he not wonderful? Let us give the greatest gift to him, for he is by far the finest creation on earth."

Epimetheus hung his head and said, "But I have already given all of the greatest gifts to the animals. I am sorry, brother. I did not stop to think."

When Prometheus heard what his brother had done, he was angry. "Now there is nothing precious to give to man. I must think of some superior and special gift to help man survive."

Prometheus was quick-witted, and soon he thought of a remarkable gift—fire! With fire man could keep warm, cook food, and have light at night. He could also forge tools to plow the earth, and weapons to defend himself against animals. But how was Prometheus to obtain fire, which belonged only to the gods?

He asked the goddess Athena to help him gain entrance to heaven, and she guided him to the blazing chariot of the sun. There Prometheus lighted a torch and then, unseen, sped back to earth to give his precious gift to mankind.

Zeus was enraged when he looked down at the earth and saw fires glowing. "Prometheus has stolen fire, which belongs to the gods alone," he roared. "And he has given our fire to man! It may make man too powerful, more powerful even than the gods. I must punish Prometheus."

Zeus acted swiftly. He had his servants Force and Violence seize Prometheus and chain him to a rock, high in the Caucasus Mountains. There, day after day, a vulture swooped down and ate his liver, which grew back daily, only to be eaten again.

But Prometheus suffered in silence, for though his body was bound, his mind and spirit were free. He did not regret his deed. He knew that not only had he fashioned a wonderful

creation—man—but he also had given him a gift that would change him from a helpless creature to master of his surroundings.

Pandora

Zeus had punished Prometheus, stealer of the fire of the gods, but he had not yet punished man for accepting the gift and using it. Now he decided to take revenge on man.

He ordered his son Hephaestus to make the first woman. After Hephaestus had created woman in the shape of a lovely goddess, the Four Winds breathed life into her.

Then each god and goddess gave her a gift to make her even more appealing to man. Aphrodite gave her great beauty, and other gods and goddesses gave her the talent for music and the power of persuasion, among other gifts. Next they adorned their creation with silvery robes and a crown of gold and named her Pandora, which means "gift-of-all."

Finally Zeus gave Pandora his gift—curiosity. He also gave her a sealed jar and warned her not to open it.

Now Zeus could put his plan to work. He sent Pandora to

earth, accompanied by the god Hermes, who gave Pandora to Epimetheus as a present from Zeus.

Epimetheus was immediately charmed by Pandora and wanted to marry her. But Prometheus, his brother, had told Epimetheus, "Zeus is full of tricks. Please, brother, do not accept any of his gifts."

Epimetheus, however, was so dazzled by Pandora's beauty and talents that he did not heed his brother's advice. Soon he and Pandora married and made a home together.

Epimetheus and Pandora lived happily, but sometimes Pandora was troubled. She would look at the sealed jar, thinking, *I wonder what is in it. Why did Zeus give it to me if he didn't want me to have what it contains?*

Every day she had to force herself to walk past the jar without opening it. *It must contain something very precious or unusual,* she thought.

At last her curiosity became so overwhelming that she ignored Zeus's warning. *I'll just take one quick look.*

She tugged and tugged at the lid of the jar, and finally it opened. Out flew a buzzing cloud of evils. Disease and envy, spite and revenge, anxiety and misfortune swarmed around her head. She batted at them and shouted, "Shoo! Shoo!" while she struggled to put back the lid. But all the evils had flown out of the house and into the world to plague mankind forever.

When at last Pandora succeeded in clamping down the lid,

only hope was left in the jar, and that was a fortunate thing. For no matter how many evils people must contend with, hope gives them the ability to endure.

Deucalion and Pyrrha and the Great Flood

Many years after Pandora had let loose the evil plagues into the world, Zeus disguised himself as a traveler and visited earth. He wanted to see how mortals—whose creation he had ordered—were behaving.

To his horror, he discovered that people were wicked and deceitful and no longer worshipped the gods. The earth and its harvest had been divided up among greedy groups who stole property from one another. People also robbed the earth of metals to make weapons, which they used to fight bloody wars with their enemies.

Zeus went back to Olympus and told the gods, "I must destroy all mankind, for people are not fit to live upon the earth. Perhaps I shall throw a huge thunderbolt at earth and burn it up. No—that might set our heaven on fire, as well. I must think of some other way to destroy all the people on earth."

At the same time, Deucalion, the son of wise Prometheus, was visiting his father, who was chained in the Caucasus Mountains. Deucalion was trying to drive away the vulture that was preying on Prometheus. But Prometheus interrupted him and said, "I have something of great urgency to tell you, my son. Because I can foresee the future, I know that Zeus, with the help of Poseidon, is preparing to drown all of mankind with a terrible flood. You must hurry home and make preparations to survive."

Deucalion did as Prometheus said. He went home and built a wooden ark that could float on water. Then he and his wife, Pyrrha, stocked the ark with herds of sheep and cattle and with food and other necessities.

Just as they had finished their preparations, Zeus unloosed the South Wind, sending dark rain clouds and howling winds to earth.

As Deucalion and Pyrrha hurried aboard their ark, the rains poured out of the heavens, filling the rivers, which rushed down the mountains. The water kept rising, higher and higher, until it covered almost the whole earth. The swirling flood swept away people and animals and buildings and crops. All was now sea, except for a few mountaintops here and there that poked their heads above the water.

Deucalion and Pyrrha were tossed about in their ark for nine dreary days and nine frightening nights, clutching each other for comfort. At last, with a bump, the ark came to rest on top of Mount Parnassus. The rains had stopped, and, little by little, the waters receded.

"There is no one left on this desolate earth," said Deucalion to Pyrrha. "I fear that we alone have survived."

They made their way to a ruined temple and thanked Zeus for saving them. They also asked him for help in their loneliness—some way for mankind to be renewed. Zeus heard them and pitied them, for he realized that they had been the only people who continued to worship the gods. He sent a Titan who

31

told them, "Cover your heads and throw behind you the bones of your mother."

Deucalion and Pyrrha were horrified. How could they do such a disrespectful thing? But after Deucalion had thought awhile, he said to Pyrrha, "I think I understand what we must do. The earth is the mother of all things, is she not?"

"Why, certainly," said Pyrrha.

"And the stones are the bones of the earth. Therefore we must cover our heads and throw earth's stones behind us."

This they did, and to their astonishment and delight, the stones thrown by Deucalion became men, and the stones thrown by Pyrrha became women.

A new race had been born, strong and hardy as stone, fit for the hard work of remaking the earth that had been wiped out by the great flood.

Triumphs of the Gods

~~~~~~

Io and Europa

Zeus, king of the gods, often fell in love with beautiful young women on earth. Naturally Queen Hera, his wife, was jealous, and Zeus thought up clever schemes to disguise his pursuit of them.

One of Zeus's loves was Io, the beautiful daughter of a river god. Whenever Zeus was with Io, he ordered a dark, thick cloud to cover the earth, concealing them. But one day Hera, sitting on her throne on Mount Olympus, said to herself, *It is unnatural for the sky to become so dark right in the middle of the day. My husband must be deceiving me again.*

She glided down to earth to surprise Zeus, but Zeus was too quick for her. He changed Io into a beautiful white cow, and when Hera arrived, he was stroking the animal. Hera, used to Zeus's crafty ways, was still suspicious, and she said to Zeus, "That is a lovely white cow. May I have her as a gift?"

Zeus knew that if he refused, he might give himself away. So he gave Io, who was now a cow, to Hera. Hera immediately

33

took the white cow to Argus, a monster with one hundred eyes, and asked him to guard her.

Io was miserable, tied up in a cave with a rope cutting into her neck, helpless and far from home. One day her father and sisters happened by, and Io mooed at them frantically, trying to tell them who she was. But of course they could not understand her bellows. When they turned to leave, she scratched her name—*IO*—in the dirt with her hoof. At last her father realized that this white cow was his beloved daughter. He tried desperately to untie her, but Argus chased him away, and Io was left to suffer alone.

Zeus, who could see all things on earth, pitied Io and sent his son Hermes to kill Argus and set Io free. But how was

Hermes to take a hundred-eyed creature by surprise? Even when Argus slept, he closed only two eyes.

Clever Hermes disguised himself as a shepherd and sat beside Argus, telling him a long tale, on and on in a monotonous tone of voice. Argus became so bored that, one by one, all of his eyes closed. Then Hermes seized his chance to kill Argus, and at last Io was free.

But Io's troubles were not over. She was still a cow, and Hera was still jealous. And when Hera saw that Io was free, she sent a gadfly to sting her repeatedly. Tormented, Io ran in a mad frenzy from mountain to seacoast and across a sea that was later called the Ionian Sea in her memory.

Finally Io reached the river Nile in Egypt. Zeus followed her there, and, after promising Hera that he would never love Io again, he changed her back into her true form—that of a lovely maiden.

*

Europa, daughter of a king, was another of Zeus's loves. She was luckier than Io, for Hera was unaware of Zeus's feelings for Europa.

One day Zeus looked down from heaven and saw a group of girls gathering flowers in a meadow near the sea. All of them were winsome, but one, called Europa, outshone the others. Zeus was smitten with love for her and immediately went to earth in disguise, just in case Hera should try to find him.

Suddenly the girls looked up and saw a herd of bulls coming toward them. "Oh, look!" cried Europa to her friends. "Have you ever seen a bull as magnificent as that one? What a rich chestnut color he is! And he has a silver circle on his brow!"

The bull, who was Zeus of course, ambled toward Europa and mooed softly. "How gentle he is!" Europa said, stroking him. Then the bull lay down at her feet, as if inviting her to climb onto his back.

Europa did so without fear. But before her friends could join her, the bull leaped up, dashed toward the ocean, and then flew over it, far out to sea. Clinging to the bull's horns, Europa looked down and saw a procession of sea gods riding on dolphins, led by Poseidon.

Europa cried out to the bull, "You, too, must be a god. And if you are, take pity on me. Do not carry me off to some strange land far from all my friends."

And the bull answered, "I am Zeus, lord of the sky, but do not be afraid, for I love you. I am carrying you to my own special island, Crete, where I was born. There I shall show myself to you as a god, and you shall bear me sons who one day will be famous and revered."

And so it happened. Europa became the mother of a great king, Minos, and also of Rhadamanthus, both judges of the dead. And Europa, after whom the continent of Europe is named, became even more famous than her sons.

~~~~~~~~

Persephone

Persephone was a high-spirited, sunny girl who loved springtime and flowers and running outdoors with her friends. She was the daughter of Demeter, goddess of the harvest, and she and her mother spent more time on earth than on Mount Olympus.

One bright day on earth Persephone was picking lilies and violets with her friends. She could not gather enough of them, though her basket was overflowing.

"Persephone, it is time to go home," called her friends.

"Just one minute longer," she called back. "I see the sweetest flower of all—a narcissus, I think. I must have one." She wandered into a far corner of the meadow, and just as she was about to pick the narcissus, she heard a deafening noise. Suddenly the earth split open at her feet. Out dashed a golden chariot pulled by black horses and driven by a stern-faced man in black armor.

Persephone dropped her basket and started to run, but the driver grabbed her by the wrist. He pulled her into his chariot, which descended back into the earth as quickly as it had risen. Then the earth closed up after it.

Persephone screamed and wept, but her friends could not hear her. Though they searched for her everywhere, all they found was her basket, with a few crushed flowers lying next to it.

Down into the earth the chariot sped, through dark caverns and underground tunnels, while Persephone cried, "Who are you? Where are you taking me?"

"I am Hades, king of the underworld, and I am taking you there to be my bride."

"Take me back to my mother," screamed Persephone. "Take me back."

"Never!" said Hades. "For I have fallen in love with you. Your sunny face and golden hair will light up my dark palace."

The chariot flew over the river Styx where Charon, the boatman, was ferrying ghostly souls across the water. "Now we are at the gate to my kingdom," said Hades, as they landed next to the huge three-headed dog who guarded it.

Persephone shivered, and Hades said, "Oh, that is Cerberus. He guards the gate so that no live mortals enter and no souls of the dead escape. Nobody escapes from the underworld."

Persephone became speechless. Never escape from this terrible place full of pale, shadowy ghosts, wandering through stony fields full of pale, ghostly flowers!

Beautiful Persephone, who loved sunshine, became Hades' queen and sat on a cold throne in his cold palace. Hades gave

her a gold crown and bright jewels, but her heart was like ice
and she neither talked nor ate nor drank.

*

Persephone's mother, Demeter, knew that something terrible
had happened to her daughter. She alone had heard Persephone's screams, which had echoed through the mountains and
over the sea.

Demeter left Olympus, disguised as an old woman, and
wandered the earth for nine days and nine nights, searching for
her daughter. She called to the mountains and rivers and sea,
"Persephone, where are you? Come back. Come back." But there
was never an answer. She did not weep, for goddesses do not

cry, but her heart was heavy. She could not eat or drink or rest, so deep was her grief.

Finally she reached a place called Eleusis, not far from the spot where Persephone had disappeared. There a prince named Triptolemus recognized her and told her this story: "Over a week ago, my brother was taking care of the royal pigs. He heard a thundering noise, and the earth opened up. Out rushed a chariot, driven by a grim-faced man. He grabbed a beautiful young girl, and down into the earth they went. They were swallowed up, along with the pigs."

"That man must have been Hades," cried Demeter. "I fear that he has kidnapped my daughter."

Demeter hurried to the sun, Helios, who sees everything. And the sun confirmed Demeter's fears. Demeter cried, "Persephone, my gay, lovely daughter, is imprisoned in the underworld, never again to see the light of day or the flowers of spring."

Then Demeter became stony and angry, and she caused the earth to suffer with her. The earth became cold and barren. Trees did not bear fruit, the grass withered and did not grow again, and the cattle died from hunger. A few men succeeded in plowing the hard earth and sowing seeds, but no shoots sprouted from them. It was a cruel year for mankind. If Demeter continued to withhold her blessings from the earth, people would perish from hunger.

Zeus begged Demeter to let the earth bear fruit again, but Demeter said, "The earth will never be green again. Not unless my daughter returns!"

Then Zeus knew that he must take action to save people from starvation. "I will see that Persephone returns," he told Demeter, "but only on one condition. She must not have eaten any of the food of the dead."

Zeus sent Hermes, messenger of the gods, down to the underworld to ask Hades for Persephone's release. When Persephone saw that Hermes had come to take her home, she became lively and smiled and talked for the first time that year.

To her delight, Hades did not protest but said, "Go, my child. Although I love you, I cannot keep you here against Zeus's will. But you must eat a little something before you leave, to give you strength for your journey." Then he gave Persephone several seeds from a red pomegranate, which was the fruit eaten by the dead. He knew that if she ate even one, she would have to return to him.

Persephone ate four seeds quickly. Then she climbed into the golden chariot and waved good-by. Hermes drove her to earth, to the temple where Demeter waited, and mother and daughter hugged and laughed and said they would never be parted again. Then Demeter remembered Zeus's warning and said, "I hope you did not eat anything while you were in the underworld."

"I was too sad to eat," said Persephone. "I didn't eat or drink all year."

"Not anything at all?" said Demeter.

"Oh, just a few little pomegranate seeds before I left," said Persephone. "Why do you ask?"

"Because, my dearest," cried Demeter, "if you have eaten any of the food of the dead, you must return to Hades."

Zeus heard the loud wails of Demeter and her daughter, and he decided to compromise. Persephone must spend just four months of each year in the underworld, one for each of the seeds she had eaten. The rest of the year she could be with her mother on earth.

That is why every year, for four months, the earth becomes cold and barren. Persephone is in the dark underworld and Demeter is overcome with grief.

And every year, when Persephone returns to earth, she brings spring with her. The earth is filled with flowers and fruits and grasses. And summer and fall, the seasons of growth and harvest, follow in their natural order. Every year Demeter and the whole earth rejoice that Persephone has returned.

Arachne

Athena, goddess of wisdom, also taught women the art of spinning and weaving. Naturally she thought she wove the most beautiful cloth in all the world. And she was furious when she heard that Arachne, a mortal, thought her own weaving was far superior.

Athena flew down to earth disguised as an old woman. She went to Arachne's hut, where wood nymphs were watching in wonder as Arachne wove an intricate pattern out of rainbow-colored threads. "I warn you," Athena said to Arachne. "Do not dare to compete with a goddess. Indeed, I advise you to ask Athena's pardon for what you said."

But Arachne said to the old woman, "I *am* the finest weaver in the world. Everybody knows that. If Athena does not believe it, let her come here and have a weaving contest with me. I am not afraid of her."

Then Athena revealed herself as a shining goddess and said, "I am Athena, and I accept your challenge. Let us begin."

Arachne paled, but she did not back down, so certain was she of her talents.

Athena and Arachne set up their looms and went to work, using every shade of every color thread, and gold and silver threads, as well. They both wove so quickly and skillfully that their shuttles seemed to fly, in and out, up and down, back and forth. The wood nymphs ran from one weaver to the other, exclaiming over the beautiful work of each.

Athena wove into her cloth scenes showing the powerful gods displeased with mortals who had challenged them. *This is a further warning to that conceited Arachne!* she said to herself. *If she does not give up, she will be sorry!*

But Arachne was lost in her own weaving and did not even notice her rival's work. Furthermore, Arachne chose to weave scenes that showed the gods' weaknesses, such as Zeus turning himself into a bull and carrying off Europa. When Athena saw

these scenes she was outraged, not only because they showed the gods in a poor light, but also because Arachne's woven web was every bit as fine as hers.

I'll not be outdone by a mere mortal, thought Athena, *and a bold, impious one at that!* And she took her shuttle and slashed Arachne's web to shreds. Then Athena touched Arachne's forehead, causing Arachne to feel guilty and ashamed.

Arachne felt so guilty and ashamed that she made a noose out of one of her strongest threads. Then she hanged herself with it.

When Athena saw poor Arachne hanging there, she pitied her a little. She sprinkled her with a magic liquid and said, "You shall not die, Arachne. Instead you shall be changed into a spider, hanging by a thread and weaving your web forever."

And Arachne shrank into a tiny spider. First her nose and ears fell off, and then her fingers turned into legs. What was left of her became her body, out of which she spins and spins the thread for her web.

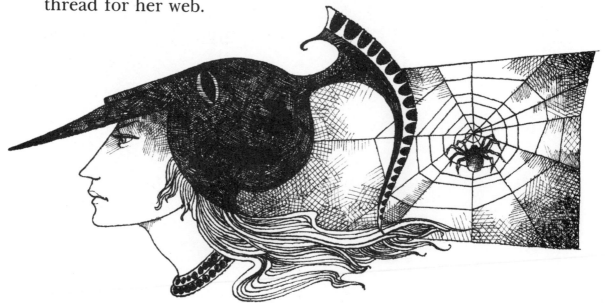

Niobe

Niobe was queen of the city of Thebes and daughter of Tantalus, who was a son of Zeus by a mortal. She had a loving husband, and together they ruled Thebes in harmony. Though Niobe had power and beauty and wealth, her greatest joy was her fourteen children—seven strapping sons and seven lovely daughters. She would have continued to be a proud, happy mother had she not defied a goddess and placed herself above her.

Niobe's downfall began at a celebration to honor Leto the Titan, mother of the goddess Artemis and the god Apollo. The people of Thebes were crowding into the temple to burn incense in Leto's honor. Suddenly Niobe appeared, and her commanding voice rang out. "Foolish people! Why do you honor Leto, when *I* am your queen? Why do you worship Leto, who has only two children, while *I* have fourteen? Leto is of no importance compared to me. Make your vows and sacrifices to *me*, not to *her*."

Leto heard Niobe's taunting words, and she called her twins, Apollo and Artemis, to a mountaintop on the island of Delos.

"Niobe, a mortal, is trying to displace *me*, a goddess," she told them. "What is more, she claims that because she has fourteen children, she is more worthy than I, a mother of two. But you, Apollo and Artemis, are a god and a goddess, far more important than all her children put together. We must teach Niobe not to belittle us."

"We must take revenge immediately," said Apollo, picking up his silver bow and arrows.

"Yes," said Artemis. "We will use our arrows to defend our mother."

And they glided to Thebes, covered by clouds, and stationed themselves on a tower. Below them was a parade ground, and there they saw Niobe's sons, richly outfitted, exercising their prancing horses.

Apollo and Artemis took aim. *Zing!* An arrow pierced the heart of Niobe's eldest son. He dropped from his horse, lifeless. Then: *Zing! Zing! Zing!* One by one, Niobe's seven sons fell to the ground and died.

Niobe heard the wailing of the bystanders and rushed to the scene, followed by her seven daughters. She knelt over her sons' bodies, screaming with grief. Yet, even in mourning, she was proud and cried to Leto, "You have not triumphed, for I am still more worthy than you. Seven of my children remain, while you have only two."

But she had hardly finished her sentence when seven more arrows felled her seven daughters.

Niobe ceased her taunting and wailing. She was so overcome with grief that she could not move or utter a word. The only sign of life in her crouching figure was her tears, which flowed without end. The gods had punished her. They had changed her into a stone that is wet with tears to this very day.

Pygmalion

Pygmalion, a talented sculptor, had vowed never to marry, for women were a great disappointment to him. He actually hated them. One day he decided to create a woman who could not possibly disappoint him, for she would be made from marble.

He worked passionately, day after day. And, little by little, his work grew into the statue of a beautiful woman. Not just any beautiful woman, but one who seemed filled with warmth and vitality and intelligence. Never had he seen such a woman. His work of art was so lifelike that Pygmalion fell hopelessly in love with his own creation.

He kissed her marble lips, but there was no response. He held her graceful hand, but it did not grasp his. He took her in his arms and talked to her, but she did not answer. How unhappy he was!

And so he pretended that his statue was alive and his own wife to love. He dressed her in a silken gown, put a string of pearls around her neck, and gave her other presents—bright flowers and shining shells. He gave her a name, Galatea, and tucked her into bed every night. Pretending helped him for a while.

But one day he said, "Oh, Galatea! If only you would come to life and be my bride, how happy I would be! For I cannot go on like this. I am wretched and miserable, loving a lifeless statue."

He continued in this state until a special day, the festival of

Aphrodite, goddess of love. On this day unhappy lovers flocked to the temple, praying to Aphrodite that their love would be returned. Pygmalion was among them, and he prayed to the goddess that his statue would come alive and return his love.

Pygmalion hurried home, filled with hope. He touched his statue. She was warm! Was he imagining things? Or was she really alive? He kissed her lips, which were suddenly soft. Then she hugged him back and smiled at him, and her eyes shone with love and joy.

And then at last she spoke to him. "You see, I *am* alive, and I am yours, for I love you every bit as much as you love me."

Aphrodite had granted his wish! And so Pygmalion and Galatea were married. Aphrodite blessed their union, and soon they had a son, named Paphos, and they all lived happily together.

Echo

Echo, a beautiful mountain nymph, was a great talker and always had to have the last word. She was a favorite of Artemis, goddess of the hunt. Together they hunted in the woods, swam in mountain pools, and caught fish for meals. But Echo's delightful

life was destroyed, all because she tried to protect her friends from Hera's wrath.

One day Hera came spying on a group of nymphs in the woods. She suspected that her husband, Zeus, was in love with one of them and hoped to find out which one he favored.

Echo did not know which nymph was Zeus's favorite, and so she started a conversation with Hera in order to let all the other nymphs escape. "Isn't it lovely here?" she said.

"Yes, indeed," Hera replied, "but I am very busy right now and have no time for talk."

"It seems to me you are busy talking," said Echo, "which is the nicest way to be busy, don't you agree?" She went on and on, and every time Hera tried to get away from her, Echo asked another question. By the time Hera got away and ran to the nymphs' pool, all the nymphs had fled.

"This is *your* doing," said Hera to Echo. "*You* kept talking to let them escape. And I shall punish you for that. You shall never be able to speak first, but shall only be able to repeat what others say. You shall always have the last word."

55

Soon after that, Echo fell in love with a handsome young hunter named Narcissus. She followed him through the woods, hoping to make him notice her. But she could not speak first and had to wait for him to speak to her.

One day her chance came. Narcissus became separated from his friends and called out, "Is anyone here?"

"Here," called Echo.

Narcissus could not see her, for she was behind a bush. He shouted, "Come," thinking she was one of his companions, and she called back, "Come."

"Let us be together," called Narcissus, for he still could not see anybody.

"Let us be together," called Echo, and she ran up to him

with her arms open, ready to embrace him. But Narcissus said cruelly, "Do not touch me. I would rather perish than let you have power over me."

"Have power over me," said Echo pleadingly, but Narcissus bounded away, leaving Echo alone and ashamed. Afterward she lived in a cave, and finally, because of her great grief, she shrank to nothing. The only thing left of her was her voice, which echoed through the mountains, repeating the words of anyone who called.

Narcissus

Many of the mountain nymphs were in love with the handsome youth Narcissus, but he paid no attention to any of them. Furthermore, he rejected them in a cruel, unfeeling way.

One of the spurned nymphs prayed to Nemesis, goddess of justice and sister of the three Fates, who determined the length of mortals' lives. The nymph asked that Narcissus, too, be rejected by a lover. Then he would know the pain that she had felt. The goddess heard the prayer and decided to make Narcissus suffer in a most unusual way.

One day, when Narcissus was hot and thirsty, he came upon a clear, undisturbed mountain pool. No animals came to drink there, no leaves fell into it, and its silvery waters reflected the sky like a mirror.

Narcissus bent over it to take a drink and saw the face of a handsome, curly-haired young man. "What a magnificent man you are!" he said. "I have never seen anyone so handsome! You must be some sort of water spirit." When he put his hands into the water to touch the beautiful youth, the water rippled and the fine face and figure disappeared. Then, when the water was still again, the spirit returned. Over and over, Narcissus tried to clasp the image in the pool, but each time it vanished. Narcissus had fallen in love with his own reflection, but he did not know it.

"Why do you flee me?" he said to the image in the pool. "Am I not handsome, too? All the nymphs adore me—why not you?"

He stayed there for days, gazing into the water, fascinated by his own beauty but unable to embrace the reflection. He became weak and pale and said to the water spirit, "I really must leave to find something to eat. Please come with me." But every time he stood up to go, the beautiful youth in the pool disappeared, too. And Narcissus could not bring himself to leave it. He could not bear to sleep, either, for if he lay down, the spirit would disappear again.

At last Narcissus wasted away and died, saying, "Alas! Alas!" Only Echo was near him, and her words, "Alas! Alas!" echoed through the mountains.

The nymphs wanted to bury him, but all that was left of his body was a beautiful flower, one that they had never seen before. They called it narcissus, in his memory.

Phaëthon

Phaëthon, a schoolboy, was being ridiculed by his schoolmates. "He says his father is the sun," they shouted. "Ha! Ha! What a silly thing to say! He only says it to make himself seem more important than we are."

"But my mother told me so," shouted Phaëthon. "And my mother would not lie."

Over and over, he asked Clymene, his mother, if she had told him the truth, and each time she would tell him that it was so. "Your father is the sun. You are descended from a god."

"But I want proof," Phaëthon would say.

"My word should be good enough for you!" his mother would answer.

Every night, before he went to sleep, Phaëthon would pretend that he was driving the chariot of the sun with its four white horses that galloped through the skies, bringing sunshine to the earth. And he would imagine his father—tall and strong and muscular, with a fiery crown on his head.

The older Phaëthon grew, the more he wanted proof that

the sun really was his father. Finally his mother said, "If you do not believe me, then go and ask your father yourself."

And so Phaëthon left his home and journeyed to the palace of the sun far away in the east.

As he approached the palace he had to shade his eyes, for the light coming from it was blinding. Gradually he became used to it and could make out the details of the palace—the gold walls, the glistening ivory roof, the brilliant red rubies around the doors, and the doors themselves, gleaming silver.

He entered and walked through shining halls until he came to the most brilliant place of all, the throne room of the sun, who was called Helios. There on a diamond-studded throne sat the powerful god. He was wearing a purple robe, and there were golden beams shimmering from his crown. Phaëthon forced himself to stare at Helios, even though it hurt his eyes dreadfully.

"What are you doing here, where no mortal has ever entered?" Helios called to him.

And Phaëthon, trembling, said, "I have come because I must find out if you are my father. Tell me yes or no, so that I can stop thinking about you night and day, year after year."

Then Helios took off his glittering crown and beckoned to Phaëthon to sit next to him on the throne. And Helios said, "It is true. I *am* your father. And to prove it to you, I shall give you anything you ask for."

"Oh, Father!" said Phaëthon, hugging him. "I am so happy."

But he could not find the words to tell his father what he wanted.

"Well, I shall make you happier still," said the god. "What can I give you? What is your heart's desire? Come, don't be shy."

"I would like to drive your chariot through the skies," said Phaëthon. "Just for one day. I have dreamed of it for as long as I can remember."

"But nobody except myself can do that!" said Helios. "Not even the other gods and goddesses, and certainly not you, a boy and a mortal. It is far too dangerous. The horses are unruly and breathe fire. The road is steep and far above the earth. Even *I* tremble when I look down. And all along the way there are frightening monsters, the Bull and the Scorpion and the Lion and the Crab."

"But I want to do it, Father," said Phaëthon. "I am not afraid."

"Isn't my fear for you proof enough that I am your father and love you?" said Helios.

But Phaëthon would not be persuaded. "If you can do it, so can I," he said.

And his father said, "I have sworn by the Styx, river of the unbreakable oath, and so I must let you do this foolish thing. You must start soon, for the stars are fading and dawn is near. But, oh, my son, drive with care."

Phaëthon climbed into the golden chariot, full of confidence, and took the reins and held them tight. The horses, already harnessed to the chariot, pawed the ground restlessly, but the god talked to them soothingly while he rubbed ointment on Phaëthon's face and neck. "This way you will be protected from the flames," said his father, and he put the fiery crown of rays on Phaëthon's head.

"Now," said Helios, "one last bit of advice. Hold the reins tight all the time, so the horses will not run away with the chariot. And do not go too high, for you might scorch the heavens, or too low, for you might scorch the earth. Be absolutely sure to stay on the middle road. Now it is time to go."

With that, the horses charged through the palace gates, carrying the chariot through the clouds. "We are going faster than the East Wind," Phaëthon shouted. "This is what I've dreamed of. I'm the king of the universe!"

Phaëthon let the horses fly freely, for the speed was exciting. He wanted to go still faster. The chariot began to sway and tip crazily, out of control. Phaëthon nearly fainted from fear and let go of the reins altogether. The horses went where they wanted, willy-nilly. One minute the chariot was high in the heavens and burned the stars of the Great and Little Bears. The next minute it plunged down toward earth and burned the mountaintops. Then it dropped even lower, setting almost the entire earth on fire—fields and forests and cities and towns. Phaëthon was nearly blinded by the smoke and could not find the reins to retrieve them. *If only I had listened to my father!* he thought. *Oh, when will this horrible nightmare end? I wish that I could die.*

At last Mother Earth called out to Zeus, "Do something quickly, before all the world is destroyed."

Zeus heard her and grabbed a thunderbolt. He aimed it at Phaëthon in the chariot and threw it expertly. It hit its target, striking Phaëthon dead. The chariot broke into pieces, and Phaëthon fell down to earth, into a river.

The sea nymphs found him there and buried him while his mother and sisters wept.

The earth smoldered for months, but gradually new trees and grass grew, and new cities and towns were built. As for Helios, he drives his new chariot through the skies every day, bringing light and warmth to the earth and its people.

Orpheus

There were nine goddesses called Muses. Born of Zeus and a Titan named Mnemosyne, each Muse presided over a different art or science.

Calliope, one of these sisters, was the inspiration of poets and musicians. She was the mother of Orpheus (a mortal because his father was one) and gave to her son a remarkable talent for music.

Orpheus played his lyre so sweetly that he charmed all things on earth. Men and women forgot their cares when they gathered around him to listen. Wild beasts lay down as if they were tame, entranced by his soothing notes. Even rocks and trees followed him, and the rivers changed their direction to hear him play.

Orpheus loved a young woman named Eurydice, and when they were married, they looked forward to many years of happiness together. But soon after, Eurydice stepped on a poisonous snake and died.

Orpheus roamed the earth, singing sad melodies to try to overcome his grief. But it was no use. He longed for Eurydice so deeply that he decided to follow her to the underworld. He said to himself, *No mortal has ever been there before, but I must try to bring back my beloved Eurydice. I will charm Persephone and Hades with my music and win Eurydice's release.*

He climbed into a cave and through a dark passage that led to the underworld. When he reached the river Styx, he plucked his lyre, and Charon, the ferryman, was so charmed that he rowed him across. Then he struck his lyre again, and Cerberus, the fierce three-headed dog who guarded the gates, heard the sweet music and lay still to let him pass.

Orpheus continued to play his lyre tenderly as he made his way through the gloomy underworld. The ghosts cried when

they heard his sad music. Sisyphus, who had been condemned to roll a rock uphill forever, stopped his fruitless work to listen. Tantalus, who had been sentenced to stand in a pool of receding water, stopped trying to quench his thirst. And even the wheel to which Ixion was tied as punishment stopped turning for one moment.

At last Orpheus came to the palace of Hades and Persephone, king and queen of the underworld. Before they could order him to leave, he began his gentle song, pleading for Eurydice.

When stern Hades heard Orpheus's song, he began to weep. Cold Persephone was so moved that, for the first time in all her months in the underworld, her heart melted.

"Oh, please, my husband," she said to Hades, "let Eurydice be reunited with Orpheus."

And Hades replied, "I, too, feel the sadness of Orpheus. I cannot refuse him."

They summoned Eurydice, and the two lovers clasped each other and turned to leave.

"Wait!" said Hades to Orpheus. "Eurydice is yours to take back to earth on one condition."

"What is that?" asked Orpheus.

"She must follow you, and you must not look back at her until you are on earth again."

"I understand," said Orpheus. "And I am forever grateful."

Orpheus and Eurydice left the underworld and made their

way through the dark passage that led to the upper world. At
last they reached the cave through which Orpheus had descended.

"I can see daylight ahead," called Orpheus to Eurydice. "We
are almost there." But Eurydice had not heard him, and so she
did not answer.

Orpheus turned to make sure that she was still following
him. He caught one last glimpse of her with her arms stretched
out to him. And then she disappeared, swallowed up by darkness.

"Farewell," he heard her cry as she was carried back to the
underworld.

Orpheus tried to follow her, but this time the gods would

not allow it. And so he wandered the earth alone. He sang his sad songs to the rocks and the trees and longed for the time when he, too, would die and be reunited with his beloved Eurydice in the underworld.

Oedipus

Jocasta, queen of Thebes and wife of King Laius, gave birth to a fine son. But the king did not rejoice, for Apollo's oracle at Delphi had told him, "You shall be killed by your own son, who shall inherit your throne."

My son must not live, thought King Laius, and he snatched the newborn baby from Jocasta's arms. Then he pierced the baby's foot with a nail and bound his feet together. He told a servant, "Take this baby into the mountains and leave him there to die."

Unknown to King Laius, a shepherd found the baby. He carried him to his master, King Polybus of Corinth, who brought him up as his son. The king named the baby Oedipus, which means "swollen foot."

When Oedipus became a young man, he, too, consulted the

oracle at Delphi, which predicted, "You shall kill your father and marry your mother."

Oedipus was horrified. *Never will I kill my kind father, King Polybus*, he thought. And to make certain that this did not happen, he left Corinth and traveled far away.

In his travels, Oedipus came to a narrow place where three roads crossed. There he met a chariot carrying a distinguished-looking older man. "Out of my way!" cried the man. "Can't you see that you are blocking the path of an important person?"

Oedipus thought, *I, too, am an important person, the son of King Polybus*, and he did not move. The man in the chariot ordered his driver, "Move ahead!" The wheels of the chariot ran over Oedipus's lame foot, hurting it badly, and Oedipus, angered, killed the driver and the older man. Oedipus had killed his father, King Laius, but he did not know it.

He continued on his way. It was not long, though, before he was stopped by a dreadful monster with the body of a lion and the head of a woman. This was the Sphinx, who lay in wait for travelers along the roads to the city of Thebes. She told each one, "If you can solve this riddle, I will let you pass. If not, I will kill you."

Many travelers had tried, failed, and perished, but Oedipus was not afraid. The terrible Sphinx asked him, "What animal goes on four feet in the morning, two feet at noon, and three feet in the evening?" Oedipus replied boldly, "Man! In babyhood he creeps on all fours, in manhood he walks upright on two feet, and in old age he walks on two feet with the aid of a third, a cane."

On hearing the correct answer, the Sphinx hurled herself over a cliff and died. The people of Thebes were overjoyed and proclaimed Oedipus their savior and king.

Not long after, Oedipus married Queen Jocasta, the widow of the murdered King Laius. Oedipus did not know that he had married his mother, as the oracle had predicted, and the two lived happily.

Years later the people of Thebes suffered a severe famine and a plague. They consulted the oracle at Delphi. The oracle answered, "Cast out the murderer of King Laius. Only then will the famine and plague be ended."

When Oedipus heard this news, he cried, "I shall find that murderer and expel him from the land."

No sooner had he said this than Teiresias, a blind seer who could predict the future, hurried to the throne room. "Oh, King Oedipus," he cried, "I have dreadful news for you and the queen."

"Speak!" said Oedipus. "For your knowledge is respected far and wide."

"Oh, King, would that I could keep the truth hidden forever. Perhaps I should not have come."

"If it is the truth, it must be spoken," said Oedipus.

"It has been revealed to me that it is *you* who have killed King Laius, your father, and married your mother."

Upon hearing this, Queen Jocasta uttered a cry of horror and killed herself. Oedipus went mad, and, seizing a pin from Jocasta's gown, he blinded himself.

Oedipus cast himself out of his kingdom and wandered from one country to another, guided by his daughter, Antigone. When he died, an old man, he was mourned only by his faithful daughter.

Bellerophon

One day Bellerophon, a courageous young man from Corinth, arrived at the court of King Iobates of Lycia in Asia. He handed the king a sealed letter, and the king greeted him cordially and welcomed him as his guest.

Many days later, the king opened the letter and read it to himself. It was from another king, and it said, "The bearer of this letter must be put to death immediately, for he has displeased my wife."

King Iobates was disturbed, for how could he put to death a guest whom he had honored at his own table? Instead he thought of a way to end Bellerophon's life without having a direct hand in his death.

He said to Bellerophon, "I have an important and difficult task for a brave warrior such as you."

"I am eager to serve you," said Bellerophon. "Tell me what I must do."

"You must slay the fire-breathing monster, the Chimera, who has been killing the people of my kingdom. She has the head of a lion, the body of a goat, and the tail of a dragon, and nobody has been able to conquer her."

"This I shall gladly attempt," said Bellerophon boldly, but actually he was shaking with fear. How could he slay such a dreadful monster?

He consulted a seer, who advised him, "You must capture the wild winged horse, Pegasus. Then mount this wonderful flying horse and do battle with the Chimera."

"Everyone has heard of Pegasus," said Bellerophon. "But how shall I capture this animal?"

"Go and sleep in the temple of Athena," said the seer, and he would say no more.

Bellerophon spent the night in the temple, sleeping fitfully, dreaming of the Chimera and of winged Pegasus. In one dream, the goddess Athena gave him a golden bridle, saying, "Use this to capture Pegasus." When Bellerophon awoke, the golden bridle was in his hand. The dream had been real! Athena had visited him during the night.

He ran out to the fields with the bridle and found Pegasus drinking from a spring. Bellerophon approached quietly, and miraculously Pegasus did not run away. Instead the horse raised his head and allowed Bellerophon to slip the bridle over it.

Bellerophon put on his armor and mounted Pegasus, and they flew up, up into the air. What a glorious feeling! They flew over fields and mountains until, below, Bellerophon sighted the Chimera, breathing fire.

He put a piece of lead on the end of his spear and directed Pegasus to circle above the monster, lower and lower, until Bellerophon was almost near enough to touch her. Then he rammed the spear into the Chimera's mouth. The monster's fiery breath melted the lead, which poured down her throat and charred her insides. Quickly the Chimera died.

The people of Lycia were overjoyed and proclaimed Bellerophon a hero. However, King Iobates still hoped that he would die. He sent Bellerophon on other dangerous adventures on his horse, Pegasus, but each time the hero was victorious.

Finally Iobates accepted Bellerophon as a hero and gave him his daughter in marriage. Many happy years followed until

Bellerophon, attempting immortality, tried to fly to Olympus on Pegasus. This angered Zeus, and he caused a gadfly to sting Pegasus. The horse reared and threw its rider, who tumbled through the sky to earth. He landed safely but became lame and blind and roamed the earth alone until his death.

Pegasus, however, flew on to Olympus and became the honored bearer of Zeus's thunderbolts.

Atalanta

One day long ago, in the mountains of Greece, a she-bear discovered a baby girl crying from hunger. The bear nursed the baby until she grew into an energetic and agile little girl. When she was older, hunters found her and brought her up. She roamed the woods with them, loving the adventure of the hunt and the free, open-air life in the forests.

Her name was Atalanta, and soon she could shoot arrows farther and more accurately than any male, outwrestle the strongest of them, and run faster than the fleetest.

Atalanta had been abandoned by her father, King Iasus, because he had wanted a son. But when he heard of her

accomplishments, King Iasus claimed her as his daughter, and she went to live in his palace.

Atalanta grew into a beautiful young woman, and one day her father said to her, "My daughter, it is time for you to take a husband."

"I shall never marry," said Atalanta. "I much prefer to roam the woods, hunting with my bow and arrow. Men make fine hunting companions, but I have no interest in them as suitors."

Nevertheless, a great many suitors pressed Atalanta to marry them. "How tiresome they are!" said Atalanta to her father.

"It is *you* who are tiresome with your silly idea of never marrying," he answered. "It is time for you to settle down, and, besides, I don't know what to tell these fine young men who seek you as a bride."

"Tell them that I shall be the bride of whichever suitor beats me in a foot race," she said, certain that *nobody* could outrun her. "And, furthermore, tell them that any man who enters the race and does not succeed in winning shall lose his life."

And so it happened that many a young prince tried to outdistance Atalanta, failed, and lost his life.

Then one day, a handsome young man named Hippomenes fell in love with Atalanta and entered the race against her. When Atalanta saw him, she almost hoped that he *would* beat her in the race and win her hand.

Hippomenes knelt down at the starting line. Silently he prayed to Aphrodite, goddess of love. "Help me, Aphrodite, for how else shall I succeed where all others have failed?"

Aphrodite heard his prayer and appeared to him, unseen by anyone else. "Take these three golden apples," she said, "and use them to your advantage during the race." And just as the race began, she whispered a plan to him.

Atalanta and Hippomenes crossed the starting line and ran forward. With a burst of speed, Atalanta drew ahead of Hippomenes, running as fast and as gracefully as a deer.

Now is the time, thought Hippomenes, and he threw one of the golden apples in front of her.

Atalanta stopped, amazed, and picked it up. *What a lovely thing*, she said to herself.

Hippomenes raced past her, while the crowd cheered him on.

Atalanta resumed the race, catching up to him and outdistancing him with ease.

Hippomenes threw the second golden apple in front of her,

and, once more, she stopped to pick up the gleaming treasure.

Again Hippomenes raced past her, and again she resumed the race. This time the finish line was near, and Atalanta was right behind him.

She must not pass me, thought Hippomenes. *This is my last chance.* He threw the third golden apple to the side of the race track, into the grass, hoping that Atalanta would stop a third time.

Atalanta hesitated. Should she pursue the golden apple when the end of the race was so near? *No,* she thought, *I must not,* and continued, her long hair flying behind her.

But just as she came abreast of Hippomenes, Aphrodite whispered in her ear, "That golden apple is the shiniest and

most precious of all. I picked it from my garden this morning, and it is for you and you alone."

Atalanta veered off the track, scooped up the apple, and returned to the race. But it was too late. Hippomenes had crossed the finish line, and the spectators were shouting, "Long live Hippomenes! Hippomenes has won! Hail to the bride and groom!"

And so the two were married, and Atalanta loved her young husband. But happiness was theirs for only a short time. They failed to pay proper respect to Aphrodite, who changed them into a lioness and lion, and yoked them to the chariot of a goddess.

The Heroes

Perseus

THE PROPHECY

King Acrisius of Argos had a beautiful daughter named Danaë, but he was not satisfied with her, for he wanted a son. He visited the oracle at Delphi to find out if he would ever have a male child. To his dismay he was told, "You shall never have a son. Furthermore, your daughter shall give birth to a son who shall take your life."

I must make certain that Danaë never has any children, said the king to himself. And he shut his daughter away from the world in a bronze house underground, so that no man would ever fall in love with her and father her child. Nobody could enter the house, for only a tiny section of the roof was open to the surface of the earth, to let in light and air.

Poor Danaë! She was all alone, week after week, with just a patch of sky to look at. Then one day a strange thing occurred. Suddenly a shower of gold rained down into her house, and that shower changed into Zeus, who declared his love for her.

Within the year Danaë bore Zeus's son, whom she named Perseus. Danaë tried to hide Perseus from her father. At last, though, King Acrisius discovered him and said to Danaë, "One day this son of yours will kill me. I cannot kill him, for that would anger his father, Zeus. But I will have the two of you sealed in a chest and tossed into the sea. If you do not survive, that will be Poseidon's fault."

"Please, Father, spare us," cried Danaë. "I will keep Perseus by my side always and make certain that he will never harm you."

But Acrisius said, "The oracle at Delphi never lies, and I must protect myself."

He ordered carpenters to make a large wooden chest. When

it was finished, he put Danaë and Perseus in it and had it thrown into the sea.

For a day and a night, Danaë cowered in the chest, holding Perseus in her arms as the waves tossed them to and fro. Then, suddenly, Danaë felt a bump, and the chest stopped moving. "We are on land," she said to Perseus. "But how can we ever get out of this sealed chest?"

Perseus was too young to understand her, and he cried and cried because he was hungry. Danaë tried to comfort him, but his wails continued, which was a good thing. A fisherman, passing by, heard the cries and broke open the chest. His name was Dictys, and he took Danaë and Perseus to his home, where he and his wife cared for them gladly, for they were childless.

Perseus grew into a strong young man and became a fisherman on that small island. He and his mother were content until Dictys's brother, Polydectes, who ruled the island, fell in love with Danaë and tried to force her to marry him. Perseus defended his mother so bravely that Polydectes decided he had to get rid of him.

Pretending he was going to marry another princess, Polydectes asked each guest to bring a wedding gift. Perseus said to Polydectes, "Alas, I am too poor to bring a gift for a ruler and his bride."

And Polydectes said, "Then I shall tell you of a gift you can win for me, but I do not know if you are brave enough to get it."

"Tell me what it is, and I promise I shall get it for you," said Perseus. "I do not lack for bravery."

"Very well," said Polydectes. "I want you to bring me the head of Medusa, the horrible Gorgon."

Perseus was trapped by his bold promise, even though he knew that this feat was impossible for one man alone. Medusa was one of the three Gorgons—huge, hideous winged creatures. Their hair was made of snakes, and their faces were so ugly that anyone who looked at them immediately turned to stone.

MEDUSA

Fortunately for Perseus, a goddess and a god overheard that conversation, and not long afterward they appeared to him and offered him their help.

First Athena flew down from Mount Olympus, holding her dazzling shield of brass. She gave it to the astonished Perseus,

saying, "You must use this as a mirror when you slay Medusa. In this way you will not look at her directly, but only at her reflection, and so you will not be turned to stone."

Perseus thanked the wise goddess and then said, "But I do not know where Medusa lives. How shall I find her?"

At that moment, Perseus saw a bright light overhead. Hermes, the messenger of the gods, flew down and landed at his side. "I shall be your guide," he said, "and also help you overcome the terrible Medusa. Here is a sword that can never be broken, not even by the hard scales of Medusa's neck."

"This is indeed a wonderful gift," said Perseus. "Now I must be on my way to slay Medusa and bring back her head."

"Not yet," said Hermes. "There are three other things you must have first: winged sandals, a magic wallet, and a cap to

make you invisible. These are guarded by the nymphs of the North, and only the Gray Women, who live in a dreary gray land, know where to find *them*. Follow me, and we will begin the long journey."

Hermes guided Perseus to the gray land, where it was always gray twilight. At last they found the shriveled old Gray Women, who had swanlike bodies and human heads, but only one eye among the three of them. Perseus and Hermes hid behind a rock and watched the Gray Women pass the eye around. Each had a turn to put it in the middle of her forehead.

"The next time the eye is passed around," said Hermes to Perseus, "you must grab it and not give it back until they tell you where to find the nymphs of the North."

Perseus waited for the right moment. Then he darted out

and snatched the eye. The Gray Women ran around blindly, shouting, "Where is our eye? Who took it?"

"*I* took your eye," Perseus said, "and I will not give it back until you tell me how to find the nymphs of the North."

Of course the Gray Women were anxious to have their eye, and so they immediately gave Perseus detailed directions. He gave them back their eye and went on his way with Hermes.

Once more they traveled far and long, this time over the ocean to the north. The nymphs of the North received them warmly and gave Perseus the three magic gifts.

Perseus put on the cap of invisibility and the magic sandals and, holding the magic wallet, flew after Hermes to the island of the Gorgons. Beneath him he could see stones in the shapes of animals and men, and he shuddered, for he knew that they had once been alive—before they had looked at the fearful Gorgons. But he was confident, now that he was armed with Hermes' sword, Athena's shield, and the three magic gifts.

Perseus hovered over the Gorgons. Fortunately he remembered to look into the mirrorlike shield at their reflections. The three hideous, winged, snake-haired Gorgons were asleep.

But which one is Medusa? he thought. *She is the only one I can kill, for the other two are immortal.* Again Athena came to his aid, saying, "That one in the middle is Medusa. Strike now, while she is asleep."

Perseus flew within inches of Medusa, his sword held ready.

Then, looking into the shield, he struck off Medusa's head with one well-aimed blow. He stuffed the head into his magic wallet, which grew large enough to hold the head with all its snakes still hissing and wriggling.

The other two Gorgons woke up when they heard the headless body of Medusa thrashing about. They flew into the air in pursuit of Perseus. But they could not see him, for he had on his cap of invisibility, and he flew away in his winged sandals, faster than the wind.

Now Perseus headed for home alone, for Hermes, his mission accomplished, had left. On his way, Perseus slew a dangerous sea monster that was about to devour a lovely princess named Andromeda. Then Perseus took Andromeda home with him, for she had agreed to be his bride.

As soon as they reached home, Perseus strode into Polydectes' palace and said to the ruler, "I have brought you the head of Medusa."

But Polydectes refused to believe Perseus. "If you even had gone *near* Medusa, you would not be here to tell the tale. What a liar you are!"

Perseus could not stand to be taunted and mistrusted. And now he realized that this cruel ruler had sent him on the chase just to get rid of him. He pulled out Medusa's head to show it to Polydectes, who turned to stone the moment he saw it.

Kind Dictys became ruler of the island, and Perseus sailed to Argos with his mother, Danaë, and his wife, Andromeda. Danaë wanted to see her father, King Acrisius, again and to be reconciled with him. But Acrisius was attending games that were being held in another city.

Since Perseus wanted to take part in the games, he journeyed to that city. There he took his turn at throwing the discus. As

the discus left his hand, a sudden wind blew it into the grandstand. It hit King Acrisius, who was a spectator, and killed him. Thus was fulfilled the prophecy of the oracle at Delphi, which had predicted that the king would be killed by his grandson.

Perseus and Andromeda were married, and they lived happily. They had a son, Electryon, who became the grandfather of another great hero, Heracles.

Heracles

THE CRIME

Heracles, called Hercules by the Romans, was the strongest man in the world. His father was Zeus, king of the gods, and his mother was Alcmena, a princess of Thebes.

Of course Hera, Zeus's wife, was jealous of Alcmena and furious with Zeus. One night, when Heracles was asleep in his crib, Hera sent two enormous snakes to kill him. Heracles saw the snakes hovering over him, ready to strike, and he reached out and grabbed them by the throat. His grasp was so strong that he strangled them to death. After this remarkable deed, it was prophesied that Heracles would become a great hero.

When he was a boy, Heracles had lessons in archery, fencing, and wrestling, and he became the best sportsman in the world. However, he had no interest in reading, writing, or music. One day he became impatient during a music lesson. Not knowing his own strength, he hit his music teacher over the head with his lyre and killed him. For some time he was sent to live in the mountains, where he could cause no more trouble.

Heracles became stronger and braver with the years. When he was only eighteen, he killed a dangerous lion in the woods near Thebes. Because of this and other heroic deeds, he was given a lovely wife, a princess named Megara.

Heracles and Megara had three sons, and he loved his wife and children dearly. But Hera, still angry, caused Heracles to go mad and kill them all. Heracles was stunned by his dreadful act and shut himself away from the world for days.

To find out how to cleanse himself of his sins, Heracles consulted the oracle at Delphi. The oracle answered, "You must go to your cousin Eurystheus, king of Mycenae, and do whatever he demands of you. Only in this way shall you be cleansed."

THE LABORS

Heracles went to Eurystheus and said, "I am your slave, and I shall do whatever you ask of me."

And Eurystheus told Heracles, "I command you to perform ten labors, all of them dangerous and nearly impossible." Jealous Hera was behind this plot, for she still wanted to see Heracles die.

"The first labor," said Eurystheus, "is to kill the lion of Nemea. This ferocious beast has such hard skin that no arrow can pierce it."

Heracles set off, full of confidence, and found the lion in the mountains. He aimed his arrows carefully. They hit the lion but bounced off its back, just as Eurystheus had said they would.

Undaunted, Heracles marched up to the roaring lion and hit it on the head with a wooden club. But the club broke apart, and the lion ran away.

Heracles caught the lion with his bare hands. Then, using a wrestling hold, he squeezed the lion until it was dead. He skinned the animal, put on its hide as a cape, and strode back to Eurystheus with the carcass.

"As you can see, I have killed the Nemean lion," said Heracles to Eurystheus.

And Eurystheus, trying to hide his awe, said, "Your second labor is more difficult and dangerous. You must kill the Hydra, a monster that has been terrorizing the neighborhood. It has nine heads that look like snakes, and it lives in a swamp in Lerna. One of its heads is immortal, and if you cut off the other eight heads, two will grow back in place of each."

Heracles set off, still confident, and found the monster in the swamp. He swung his club at its eight heads, one after another. But every time he smashed one of the heads, two grew in its place. To make matters worse, Hera sent a huge crab to bite his foot. But Heracles was not distracted from his task. He kicked the crab away and, with the help of his charioteer, used a torch to burn off the Hydra's eight mortal heads. That way, new ones could not grow again.

Next Heracles cut off the immortal head with his sword and

buried it under a rock. He went back to Eurystheus and said, "I have killed the Hydra. People will have no more to fear from it. Now, what is my third labor?"

And Eurystheus, amazed, said, "You must go to the forest of Cerynitia and bring back a white deer with horns of gold. This deer belongs to the goddess Artemis, who protects it. And you must bring it back alive, which is even more difficult than killing it."

Heracles set off to find the white deer, not allowing himself to think of failure. After all, he had completed the first two nearly impossible labors!

For a whole year, he chased the fleet-footed deer through the forest of Cerynitia. Finally he shot an arrow that pierced its leg. The deer fell, and Heracles hoisted it up onto his shoulders and traveled the long way back to Eurystheus.

Again Eurystheus was amazed, but still he did not show it. He sent Heracles off to perform his fourth labor, saying, "This time you must capture the boar of Mount Erymanthus and bring it back alive. No hunter has conquered this gigantic beast, for its sharp tusks can spear a man to death, and its skin is so tough that no arrow can penetrate it."

But Heracles accomplished this task with ease. He chased the boar through the snow-clad mountains into a deep snowdrift. The tired animal could not move, but Heracles, full of vigor, stamped through the drift and caught up with the boar quickly.

He tied it up, then hoisted the heavy burden onto his strong shoulders and brought it back alive.

Eurystheus was so frightened by the huge boar that he hid in a big brass jar.

Now it was time for Heracles to perform his fifth labor. Eurystheus said to him, "This labor is not as difficult as killing or trapping an animal, but it is much more distasteful. Wealthy King Augeas has a yard filled with thousands of bulls, and he has not had their dung cleared away for thirty years. You must clean the yard in just one day."

Heracles used both his strength and his wits this time. He swung his club at the walls of the cattle yard and made huge holes in them. Then he changed the courses of two rivers, which swept through the holes and carried all the mess along with them. It took him only an hour to accomplish this.

"That was easy," said Heracles to Eurystheus, and Eurystheus, annoyed, said, "The sixth labor is a great deal harder. I very much doubt that you can complete it. You must go to the marsh where the Stymphalian birds live and get rid of them. They have brass feathers that they shoot at people, and their long beaks can peck through a man's shield."

Heracles set off. When he reached the marsh, the birds were hiding. But fortunately the goddess Athena flew down and said, "Here is a rattle. Shake it and you will see what happens."

Heracles shook the rattle. It made such an ear-splitting noise that hordes of the frightened birds flew away. The rest of the birds flew up in the air, and he killed them with his arrows. Soon he was back, telling Eurystheus of his conquest.

"And what is my seventh labor?" Heracles asked.

"You must go to the island of Crete," said Eurystheus, "and catch a terrifying bull that is mowing down farmers and their families and destroying their barns and their crops. Bring him back to me alive, though I am certain you cannot do it."

Heracles sailed off to Crete. When he arrived, he chased the bull through the mountains for many days. At last the bull tired, and Heracles wrestled him to the ground, tied a rope around his neck, and led him onto the ship.

Eurystheus could not believe his eyes when he saw the savage bull being led tamely by Heracles. He thought long and hard to devise a still more difficult labor.

"Your eighth labor," said Eurystheus, "is to bring me the man-eating mares. They belong to the wicked King Diomedes of Thrace, who has been feeding his guests to these wild creatures."

Heracles sailed to Thrace and overcame the wild mares. He led them to the ship, but the king and his troops ran after him. Heracles battled them all with his club and, after hitting King Diomedes on the head, fed him to the mares. Then he sailed back to the mainland with the mares and brought them to Eurystheus.

"Now I have accomplished eight labors," said Heracles. "What is the ninth?"

Eurystheus was getting angrier and angrier at Heracles' astonishing successes, which only served to make him more famous.

Eurystheus thought of a still more difficult labor and said, "My daughter wishes to own the golden girdle of Hippolyte,

queen of the Amazons. The Amazons are brave women warriors, clad in helmets and skins of wild beasts. They are fully armed and ride spirited horses into battle. I dare you to frighten them off."

Heracles sailed to the land of the Amazons. To his surprise, Queen Hippolyte was perfectly willing to give him her golden girdle. But as she stepped on board the ship to take it off, Hera, posing as an Amazon, told the other warriors that Heracles was going to kidnap their queen. They stormed the ship, and Heracles, thinking that Hippolyte had plotted the attack, swung his club at the queen, killing her with one blow. He took the golden girdle, battled the army of Amazons, and sailed away unharmed.

When Eurystheus saw the golden girdle, he thought, *This Heracles is indeed an unbeatable man, but I must think of a labor that is beyond his powers.*

At last he said to Heracles, "Your tenth labor is to bring me the cattle of King Geryon from an island near Spain. King Geryon is a horrible monster with three bodies on one pair of legs, and his cattle are guarded by his two-headed dog."

Heracles strode off, thinking only of victory on his long hike to Spain. When he reached the area where Spain and Africa were connected, he decided to erect a monument in memory of his journey. He swung his heavy club and cut the land in two, forming the channel that we call the Strait of Gibraltar. The cliffs on either side are called the Pillars of Hercules to this day.

Then Heracles sailed to Geryon's island. When he landed, the two-headed dog rushed at him, angry and snarling. Heracles killed the dog with his club and loaded the cattle onto his ship. Geryon came running after Heracles, but Heracles shot each of his three bodies with arrows and set sail for the mainland.

He drove the cattle back to Greece and said to Eurystheus, "I have completed the ten labors. Now you must set me free."

But Hera whispered to Eurystheus, and Eurystheus repeated her words to Heracles. "Since you had help in performing two of the labors, you must perform two more."

Heracles protested, but Eurystheus said, "Your charioteer helped you light the torch with which you conquered the Hydra,

and the rivers, not you, washed clean the cattle yard of King Augeas."

Heracles was angry, but he had no choice and waited to hear what his eleventh labor was to be.

"Your eleventh labor," said Eurystheus, "will be the most difficult by far. You must bring me the golden apples of the Hesperides."

Heracles did not know where to find the golden apples that were guarded by Atlas's daughters, the Hesperides, and by a dragon with one hundred heads. However, he set off confidently on his eleventh and most difficult labor.

Soon after he had begun his search, he came upon Prome-

theus, whom Zeus had had chained to a rock in the Caucasus Mountains. Heracles smashed the chains with his club and freed Prometheus.

Prometheus said, "You have done me a great service. What can *I* do to help *you*?"

"Please tell me where to find the golden apples of the Hesperides."

And Prometheus told him, "Journey to Mount Atlas in Africa, where the Titan Atlas holds the heavens on his shoulders." Then he warned him, "Do not pick the golden apples yourself, for if a mortal picks them, he will die. They belong to Hera and were a gift to her from Mother Earth."

Heracles thanked him, and after many days' journey he came upon Atlas, who was bent from the weight on his shoulders.

Heracles said to Atlas, "Will you do me a favor? Pick the golden apples from the secret garden of the Hesperides and give them to me. While you are gone, I will hold up the heavens for you."

And Atlas agreed, thinking that he could give his heavy burden to Heracles forever. Carefully Atlas shifted the great weight onto Heracles' shoulders. Then he went off to the garden of the Hesperides.

What a long time he is taking! thought Heracles. *Maybe the dragon has killed him.*

But at last Atlas returned, carrying the gleaming apples.

"Thank you very much," said Heracles. "Now I can take the golden apples to Eurystheus."

But Atlas said, "Oh, don't bother. *I'll* take them for you," and he walked away.

Heracles thought, *He is trying to trick me, leaving me with his heavy burden,* and he called out to Atlas, "Just hold up the sky for a minute while I make a pad for my shoulders. They are getting sore."

Atlas agreed, putting down the apples and taking the sky on his shoulders. Heracles picked up the apples and ran off with them, while Atlas roared and raged at his own stupidity.

Eurystheus had not expected Heracles to return with the

golden apples. When he saw them he said, "I cannot imagine how you picked them."

And Heracles said, "It was no trouble at all."

This enraged Eurystheus so much that he thought up an even more difficult and dangerous twelfth labor. "You must capture Cerberus, the three-headed dog who guards the gates of the underworld." And he said to himself, *This labor is surely an impossible one.*

But Heracles was not daunted. He descended to the underworld and asked King Hades for permission to borrow Cerberus.

"Certainly," said Hades, "if you can capture him without using any weapons." Hades felt sure that Heracles could not meet his terms.

But Heracles crept up on Cerberus and squeezed him with his bare hands, just enough to take the fight out of the dog.

When Eurystheus saw Heracles carrying the savage, three-headed dog, he was terrified. "Take him back!" he cried.

"Not unless you promise me that my labors have been completed."

"I give you my word," said Eurystheus. "You are indeed a hero of great courage and strength. You have completed your labors honorably."

At last Heracles was cleansed of his sin and free to roam the earth, ridding it of giants and monsters wherever he went.

Jason

THE ARGONAUTS

Jason was the son of King Aeson of Iolcus and rightful heir to the throne. But before Jason was born, King Aeson's half brother, Pelias, had overthrown the king and imprisoned him.

Jason's mother pretended that her son had died at birth. And she took him away secretly to be brought up by Chiron the centaur, a creature who was half horse and half man. If King Pelias had known of Jason's existence, he would surely have put the boy to death.

Even though Pelias knew nothing of Jason, he could not rest. For an oracle had warned him that he would be killed by a relative and that he must guard against a man wearing one sandal.

Many years later, a handsome young man with curly, golden hair came walking into the marketplace at Iolcus. He was wearing a leopard's skin and only one sandal. He had lost the other while carrying an old woman across a river.

When King Pelias saw the tall stranger with one sandal, he was instantly afraid. Surely he was the man about whom the oracle had warned Pelias.

"What is your name?" said King Pelias. "And why have you come to my kingdom?"

"I am called Jason," said the stranger. "I have come to claim the throne, for my father is your half brother, and I am the rightful king of this land. I do not wish to quarrel with you. You may keep all the riches of the kingdom, but I must have the title of king, for it belongs to me."

King Pelias thought quickly and said, "I shall not quarrel with you. The throne shall soon be yours. But first you must do one thing. Bring back the Golden Fleece from the kingdom of Colchis. It hangs on a tree there and is guarded by a dragon that never sleeps. This ram's fleece of gold belongs to *our* kingdom, and only a strong, fearless man like you can recover it. When you return with it, I shall yield my throne."

King Pelias was sure that nobody could survive such a dangerous quest, but Jason did not know this. "What a fine

adventure it will be," said Jason. "I accept the challenge gladly. I shall choose a group of brave young heroes and have a sturdy ship constructed at once."

Jason asked Argus, a master shipbuilder, to build him a great ship with fifty oars. Then he sent envoys to every palace in Greece, asking for volunteers to help capture the Golden Fleece. The ship was called the *Argo*, and the fifty volunteers, called Argonauts, included heroes such as Heracles and Orpheus.

As the group rowed away, Jason, the leader, prayed to Zeus to bless the dangerous journey. The strong Argonauts pulled their oars, and the ship sped through the waves.

After a while, Heracles called out, "Let us have a contest to see which of us can row the longest."

"Agreed!" cried the others, and they rowed for many long hours until, one by one, they grew tired and had to give up. Only Jason and Heracles continued. Finally Jason fainted from overexertion, and Heracles' oar broke in two.

The Argonauts pulled their boat onto a sandbar in a river so that they could rest. And Hylas, Heracles' squire, went ashore to find drinking water. A long time passed, and he did not return. Heracles went ashore and ran through the forest, calling his squire's name, but he could not find him. A water nymph who had fallen in love with Hylas had pulled him down into the spring where she lived. Heracles did not know this and continued searching for Hylas.

When Heracles did not return, the Argonauts combed the

shore for hours, calling, "Heracles! Heracles! We must leave."
At last Jason made the difficult decision to set off without him,
for the wind was in their favor.

Before long the Argonauts came to a kingdom where the
withered, starved ruler, named Phineus, pleaded for their help.
"Because I am able to predict the future, Zeus has punished me.
Every time I begin a meal, he sends two horrible flying creatures,
the Harpies, to snatch some of my food and make the rest smell
so foul that I cannot eat it."

"We are ready to serve you," said Jason, pitying the man.
"Tell us what we must do."

"Only two of your men, the sons of Boreas, the North Wind,
can drive them off," said Phineus.

The sons of Boreas stepped forward with their swords ready.
Then the Argonauts put dinner in front of Phineus. The Harpies
flew down, snatched the food with their sharp claws, and flew
off with it. But this time the sons of Boreas flew after them and

slashed at them with their swords, chasing them far away. "They won't bother you anymore," they said to Phineus.

"I cannot thank you enough," he replied. "You have saved my life. And now I am going to help *you*, for I know that you must row through the dangerous Bosphorus strait on your way through the Black Sea to Colchis."

Phineus gave them invaluable advice, and the Argonauts set forth once more. At last they sighted the huge, jagged rocks called the Symplegades, or Clashing Islands, that guarded the entrance to the Bosphorus. Phineus had told them, "When a ship tries to go between these floating rocks, the rocks move together and smash the ship to pieces. There is only one way to get through. Let a dove fly before you, and when the rocks crush its tail, row through with all your might. Thus you will pass as the rocks separate before clashing again."

Jason let the dove go. Just as Phineus had predicted, the rocks smashed together, crushing the tip of the dove's tail. Then

Jason gave the command: "Row!" The Argonauts did, and as the huge rocks drew apart, the *Argo* slid through safely.

Jason looked back and saw the rocks smash together again. But they crushed only the very tip of the ship, which was quickly repaired. Afterward the rocks became rooted, and ever since the passageway has been safe for sailors.

THE GOLDEN FLEECE

The Argonauts rowed through the Black Sea for days. At last they anchored at Colchis, tired but excited. "Somewhere in this land, the Golden Fleece is guarded by a fierce dragon," said Jason. "I do not know how we shall find it, but find it we will. First, though, we must refresh ourselves with a long sleep."

While the Argonauts slept under the stars, Hera and Athena discussed them on Mount Olympus. "We must help Jason," they

said to each other, for Jason was one of their favorite mortals. Then they both had the same idea. "Let us ask Aphrodite for her aid."

Aphrodite, goddess of love, was always happy to use her powers, and she said to her son, Eros, "I shall give you a shining toy, a ball of gold, if you do what I ask."

"Only ask," said Eros, anxious to have the toy.

"You must make the daughter of the king of Colchis fall in love with Jason. Her name is Medea, and she is a witch. Only Medea can help the Argonauts with their dangerous mission."

Eros prepared to fly down to earth while the Argonauts made their way to the palace of King Aeëtes of Colchis. The king greeted them courteously, as did his daughter, Medea. But King Aeëtes felt uneasy. He asked Jason who he and his companions were and why they had come to him. Jason replied, "We are all brave men of Greece, and we have come to ask you for the Golden Fleece. Ask us any service, and we shall perform it for you in exchange for the fleece."

King Aeëtes had no intention of handing over his most precious possession. And so he thought of an impossible task for the Argonauts to perform.

He said to Jason, "I shall be happy to give you the Golden Fleece. But first you must yoke to a plow two bulls that breathe fire. Then you must plow the field, and into the furrows of the earth you must sow the teeth of a dragon. These teeth are seeds from which a crop of armed men shall grow. They shall attack you and, single-handed, you must mow them down."

Jason said, "This I shall do tomorrow," although he could not imagine how he would accomplish such an impossible task.

At that moment Eros flew down to Colchis. Quickly he shot an arrow of love into Medea's heart, and from that time she could not take her eyes off Jason.

Medea longed to help Jason with her magic, but she tried desperately to put aside her thoughts of him. Was he not, after all, an enemy of her father?

That night she twisted and turned in bed, torn between her love for Jason and her loyalty to her father. But Eros's arrow

had done its job well, and at last she sent her servant to bring Jason to her.

In the middle of the dark night, Medea declared her love for Jason and said, "If you promise to take me as your wife, I shall help you." And Jason clasped the lovely sorceress in his arms, promising to wed her.

Then Medea said to him, "Here is a magic ointment. Spread it over your body and your weapons. It will protect you from the fire-breathing bulls and the armed men who will spring up when you have sown the dragon's teeth." She also gave him a magic stone to throw among the armed men. "Now go, for there is not much time before daylight."

The next morning Jason spread the magic ointment on his body and on his spear and his shield. Then he went to the field where King Aeëtes and his warriors awaited the spectacle.

"Jason will be killed by the fire-breathing bulls," said the king's son, Apsyrtus.

"That is certain," said the king. "What a fool he is to undergo this ordeal."

Jason strode out onto the field, and the two fire-breathing bulls were set loose. Jason ran after them, grabbed them both by the horns, and yoked them to the plow.

"The bulls breathe fire on Jason, yet they do not even singe him," said Apsyrtus. "How can this be?"

"It is indeed strange," said the king. "But he will not be able to withstand the armed warriors who will spring up when he sows the dragon's teeth."

Jason drove the bulls across the field. The plow cut furrows in the earth. Into these Jason sowed the dragon's teeth. Instantly

an army of fierce armed men sprang up and ran to attack Jason. But Jason threw the magic stone into their midst, and the men began killing one another with their spears.

King Aeëtes was furious. He said to his son, "Jason shall never have the Golden Fleece. Go and call our army together. Tonight, when he expects me to give him the treasure, we will attack his band of men on board their ship."

Because Medea was a sorceress, she knew her father's plan. That night she stole to Jason's ship and said, "My father is planning to prevent you from capturing the Golden Fleece. You must seize it now, before he attacks you. I shall come on board and lead you to the sacred grove where the Golden Fleece hangs."

The heroes rowed quietly as Medea guided them. "Now!" she said suddenly. "Stop here and pull up your ship on shore."

They did as she said. Then Medea and Jason crept ashore to the sacred grove. There they saw the Golden Fleece hanging

from a tree and glistening in the moonlight. A huge, hissing dragon guarded it, but Medea sneaked up and sang it a soothing, magical lullaby. Soon the dragon was fast asleep.

Jason snatched the Golden Fleece, and he and Medea ran back to the ship. The heroes rowed away as fast as they could. And not until they were several miles out to sea did Jason show them the Golden Fleece. They all marveled at the hard-won prize and praised Medea for her help in gaining it. "But how will Medea get back to the palace?" they asked.

"She is not going to leave us," said Jason. "For I have promised to marry her as soon as I can."

It was not long before King Aeëtes learned that Jason and the Argonauts had rowed away with the Golden Fleece and his daughter, Medea. The king sent Apsyrtus with an army to pursue them.

Once again Medea saved the Argonauts with her trickery. She sent a message to Apsyrtus, asking him to meet her on an island. There she would give him the Golden Fleece, and then she would return with him to their father.

Jason accompanied Medea that night. When Apsyrtus arrived, Jason slew him with one stroke of his sword. Medea's robe was covered with her brother's blood, but she was so hardhearted that she did not even grieve over him.

Apsyrtus's army, now leaderless, gave up. Jason and Medea rejoined the Argonauts, and they sped toward home in the *Argo*.

THE RETURN HOME

On the way, they had many adventures. They were nearly entrapped by the Sirens, beautiful sea nymphs whose singing charmed sailors and caused them to jump into the sea. But Orpheus played his lyre so sweetly that it drowned out the Sirens' songs.

Later the *Argo* was nearly destroyed by two monsters. One, Scylla, had been a beautiful young girl before an enchantress turned her into a dreadful creature. Now she had six heads, each on its own long, snakelike neck, and dogs' heads grew from her waist. Scylla devoured those who passed her, while Charybdis, the other monster, drew huge amounts of water into her mouth, then poured them out again, causing a dangerous whirlpool. But as the ship passed through the narrow passage guarded by the monsters, Hera sent sea nymphs to protect it from their clutches.

At Crete a bronze giant threw rocks at the *Argo*, trying to sink it. But Medea bewitched the creature, and he fell over and died.

Finally the *Argo* landed safely at Iolcus. "Home at last!" shouted the victorious Argonauts as Jason stepped ashore to present the Golden Fleece to King Pelias.

But Jason's joy was short-lived. To his horror, he learned that King Pelias had killed his father and that his mother had died soon after of grief.

Jason enlisted Medea's help to punish Pelias. Medea told Pelias's daughters that she had the power to make Pelias young again. In order to persuade them that she could bring this about, she cut up and boiled an old sheep together with some magic herbs. Soon a young lamb leaped out of the cauldron.

The daughters of Pelias were convinced. They asked Medea to cast a spell to put their father to sleep. Then they cut up Pelias and put him in the boiling water. But this time Medea did not add the magic herbs, and poor Pelias did not return to life.

The prophecy that Pelias would be killed by a relative was thus fulfilled.

But the dreadful Medea had no power to keep Jason's love. He fell in love with a princess of Corinth and determined to marry her, despite all that Medea had done for him.

Medea was enraged at Jason's heartless desertion. On the wedding day, she sent Jason's bride a beautiful robe that she had sprinkled with poison. When the princess put it on, it burst into flames, killing her.

Then Medea killed her own two children, whose father was Jason, for she knew that life held nothing for them after her terrible deed. Her children would be slaves in Corinth, at best, or put to death, at worst. Medea fled in her chariot drawn by

dragons. And Jason was left a lonely man, mourning for his young bride-to-be and his beloved children.

Jason was no longer in the favor of the gods, for he had broken his word to Medea so that he could marry another. He became a friendless, homeless old man, and one day, when he returned to gaze at his ship, the *Argo*, the prow fell on his head, and he died.

Long after Jason's death, the Golden Fleece hung in a temple of Zeus, and all of Greece could see it and remember the remarkable feats of Jason and his heroic band of Argonauts.

Theseus

THE BANQUET

Princess Aethra of Troezen was secretly married to King Aegeus of Athens. Theseus, their son, grew up in his mother's palace, not knowing who his father was. He hoped that his father was a god, *for then*, he thought, *I am bound to become a hero, like my idol, cousin Heracles.*

On his sixteenth birthday, Theseus's mother said, "My son, you have grown into a fine young man. Now you might be strong enough to perform a feat that will enable me to reveal your father's name."

"Who *is* my father, and what is this feat?" asked Theseus, following his mother into the woods.

"Soon you will have the answer," his mother replied. She stopped at a huge rock. "Can you roll away this heavy rock?"

"I shall try," said Theseus. He put his shoulder to the rock and heaved his body against it. The rock rolled away. Underneath it lay a pair of sandals and a glittering sword.

"Whose are these?" said Theseus, mystified. "How did they come to be under this rock?"

"They belong to King Aegeus of Athens, who is your father. He hid them here for you to find when you became a strong

young man. Once you had found them, I was to tell you his name and send you to Athens to claim him as your father."

Theseus was overjoyed at this news. "I shall start immediately," he said, and he returned to the palace to prepare for his journey.

His grandfather, the king of Troezen, said, "You must go by sea, Theseus. It is the safer way, for the roads are full of evil bandits."

"I do not care for safety and ease," said Theseus. "How, then, could I prove myself a hero?"

Theseus took the long road to Athens, and he slew the evil bandits who had made that road a menace to travelers.

When at last he arrived in Athens, the streets were thronged with well-wishers, for the people of that city had heard of the young traveler's brave deeds. Among them was an envoy of King Aegeus, who said to Theseus, "I have an invitation for you from King Aegeus. He is giving a banquet tonight in your honor."

Theseus accepted gladly, thinking, *The king does not yet know that I am his son. I shall surprise him at the banquet tonight.*

But the king's wife, the sorceress Medea, knew who Theseus was, for she had magical powers. She also knew that once Aegeus was united with his son, she would lose her position of influence. So she told the king that Theseus was planning to dethrone him and declare himself king, and she persuaded Aegeus to poison Theseus at the banquet.

It was a sumptuous dinner, and Theseus was in high spirits, waiting for the right moment to spring his surprise on his father. *I shall reveal my secret when he toasts my good health,* Theseus thought.

Finally the moment came. Medea handed Theseus a goblet of wine, and King Aegeus lifted his goblet to propose a toast to the young hero. Theseus pulled out his father's sword, laid it on the table, and raised the poisoned drink to his lips. His father, seeing the sword, realized Theseus was his son. He rushed over to him and dashed the goblet from Theseus's hand. "My son!" he cried. "At last you have come!"

Father and son embraced, and all of Athens welcomed the heir to the throne. Medea was banished to Asia, where she could do no harm.

THE MINOTAUR

Theseus could have lived safely and comfortably in his father's palace until he became king of Athens. But such was not his nature. He wanted life to be a challenge, and it was not long before that challenge presented itself.

Every nine years, the people of Athens had to send seven youths and seven maidens to King Minos of Crete. He fed these fourteen young people to the ferocious Minotaur, a creature that was half bull and half man. This was the payment that

Minos demanded for the loss of his only son, who had died while carrying out a perilous deed for King Aegeus. If the Athenians had not sent the young people to Crete, King Minos would have sent his troops to destroy Athens.

It was now time to choose fourteen victims from a group who awaited their fate in the main square of Athens. King Aegeus drew lots and read the names of the doomed young people, while their mothers and fathers screamed with grief.

Just before the fourteenth lot was drawn, Theseus shouted, "Stop! I shall be the fourteenth person to go to Crete, and I shall kill the Minotaur and end these horrible sacrifices."

Theseus's father protested, saying, "Even if you kill the Minotaur, you will never find your way out of the labyrinth where the Minotaur lives. It is a maze of winding passages underneath King Minos's palace, constructed by Daedalus, a clever inventor."

But Theseus stood firm and boarded the ship with black sails that was bound for Crete. As he waved farewell to his father, he called, "When I return home victorious, I shall hoist white sails, and you will know that I have slain the Minotaur and am returning to you alive."

As the ship sailed away, Theseus comforted the tearful young victims on board. "Take heart," he said. "I shall go into the labyrinth first and overcome the Minotaur. Athens shall never sacrifice another victim."

When the ship arrived at Crete, the fourteen youths and maidens were driven from it like cattle and paraded before King Minos. Ariadne, the king's lovely daughter, was at his side. As soon as she saw the strong, clear-eyed Theseus, she fell in love with him. At the same time, Theseus was smitten with love for her. Their eyes met, and Ariadne thought, *I must think of a way to save him from his terrible fate.*

That night Ariadne crept out of her bedroom and tiptoed to the rooms where Theseus and his companions were guarded. "I have come to comfort the victims on their last night on earth," she said to the guard, and he let her pass.

She entered the room full of sobbing young people. Only

Theseus was dry eyed, praying to the gods to protect him and give him strength to kill the Minotaur with his bare hands.

Ariadne approached him and said, "I have fallen deeply in love with you. If you will promise to marry me, I shall give you something that will help you find your way out of the labyrinth."

"And I have fallen in love with you," said Theseus, "and shall marry you gladly. Aphrodite must have heard my prayers and sent you to me."

They embraced, and then Ariadne gave Theseus a ball of thread. "This will guarantee your escape from the labyrinth. Fasten one end of the thread to the post by the door as you enter. Then, as you go into the maze, let the ball of thread unroll. After you have killed the Minotaur, you can find your way out by following the thread. But, oh, I wish I had a sword to give you, for I fear that the monster will take your life."

"Have no fear," said Theseus. "Thanks to your love and this

precious ball of thread, my strength and courage have doubled. Now go, before the guard becomes suspicious."

"Just one more thing," said Ariadne. "The Minotaur will still be asleep when you enter the labyrinth. Go quietly, and take it by surprise."

After they had said good-by, Theseus slept for a few minutes. He awoke refreshed and confident.

When the guard marched into the room to summon the first victim, Theseus stood up, hiding the ball of thread under his cloak. The guard led him down three flights of steps, underground, to the door of the labyrinth. He then opened the door quickly, thrust Theseus into the dark passageway, and shut the door firmly.

Theseus could not see in the blackness, but his fingers found the doorpost. He tied the end of the thread around it. Then, slowly and quietly, he felt his way along the twisting passageway. Here and there, light came through a chink in the ceiling. His eyes became accustomed to the darkness, and he saw the path split—one way to the right, one way to the left. Which way should he choose? He had very little time to surprise the Minotaur while it was still asleep.

Though I cannot see it, perhaps I can hear the Minotaur, he thought. *Then I shall know which path to follow.* He stood quietly, listening for the monster's breathing.

He heard a low, rumbling sound and went toward it.

Whenever the maze passage branched off, he listened quietly and followed the sound.

Now the sound of the Minotaur's breathing was a loud rumble. It grew louder and louder, until Theseus had to hold his ears for a moment to get relief from the noise. His head ached, but he crept still nearer.

Suddenly the passageway branched off in three directions. A faint light came from one of them, straight ahead. He took that path. As the light became brighter, the noise became louder until finally, in the center of the labyrinth, Theseus came upon the dreadful beast.

The monster was sound asleep, and fire shot out of its nostrils. Theseus crept up behind it. The Minotaur stirred, changing its position.

Theseus climbed up the rocky wall behind the Minotaur and stood poised over the monster. He put down the ball of thread on a ledge. Then, summoning all his strength, he leaped onto the Minotaur's back and strangled it with his bare hands, tighter and tighter, until its breathing stopped and the fire went out.

Then he groped in the dark for the ball of thread. Where was it? Had he lost it?

At last he found it. He held the ball in one hand and, with the other, felt for the thread that had unwound. He followed it, winding it up as he went, and, twisting and turning, he found his way back to the entrance of the labyrinth.

When Theseus opened the door, there stood Ariadne, waiting. They embraced quickly, and then, after two of the

Athenians knocked down the guard, all fourteen youths ran to the ship with Ariadne. It was not yet daylight, and they crept aboard undetected. They untied the ship from the pier and rowed away from Crete.

When they reached the island of Naxos, they all went ashore to find food and drink. Ariadne, exhausted, fell asleep, and Theseus abandoned her there. He did so because the god Dionysus had appeared to him in a dream and threatened him, for the god loved Ariadne himself.

Poor Ariadne was desolate when she woke up alone and saw the ship, with her beloved Theseus at the helm, far away on the horizon. But Dionysus came to her and comforted her, and soon he won her love.

Theseus and his companions sailed on to Athens. Theseus was distraught at having left Ariadne and at the same time excited to be returning home. For both reasons, he forgot to change the black sails to white, the signal of victory.

His father stood on a cliff near Athens, waiting for the ship to return. At last he sighted the black sails. He cried out, "Theseus, my son, has been killed by the Minotaur." Grief stricken, the king jumped off the cliff into the sea and drowned. That sea is called the Aegean Sea in his memory.

Theseus inherited his father's title—king of Athens. But he believed that people should govern themselves. And so he resigned from his position and let the Athenians vote for their

representatives and rule themselves in this way. Athens became the first true democracy, and Theseus was remembered as a great hero and a wise man.

DAEDALUS

When King Minos heard that Theseus had killed the Minotaur and escaped from the laybrinth, he roared to his soldiers, "Daedalus must have helped Theseus escape, for only he knows the plan of the labyrinth. Take Daedalus and his young son, Icarus, up to the tower and bolt the door. They shall be imprisoned there forever."

But Daedalus, the great architect and inventor who had designed the labyrinth, did not lose hope, though he was locked in the gloomy tower. "The king cannot imprison my mind," he said to Icarus. "I shall think of a way to escape."

"But even if we get out of this tower, King Minos will find us and lock us up again," said Icarus. "We cannot leave Crete by ship, for all ships are searched before they leave. And soldiers patrol the land."

"There is another way open to us," said Daedalus. "The sky! If we could fly, they would never be able to follow us."

"Fly!" said Icarus. "Only birds can fly. No human has ever done so."

"But we can learn from the birds," said Daedalus. "Come with me to the roof."

Icarus followed his father, and together they studied the birds flying past the tower.

"If *we* had wings made of feathers, we, too, could fly," said

Daedalus. "We must catch the birds and use their feathers to make wings for ourselves."

Soon they had a whole pile of feathers of all colors, for they took only a few from each bird, not wanting to cripple them. Daedalus laid the feathers on the floor, according to size. Then he put the smallest feathers in a row, the middle-sized feathers in another row overlapping the first, and the largest feathers overlapping those.

Icarus watched in wonder as the man-sized wings took shape. "But how will you hold the feathers together?" he asked.

Daedalus pulled out a spool of thread and a large needle from his pocket, which was filled with odds and ends. "An inventor must always have his tools at hand," he said, and he set about sewing the large feathers together.

Next Daedalus pulled out some wax and softened it to hold the smaller feathers to the larger ones. When that was done, he lifted the man-made wings and bent them so that they curved

like the wings of a bird. He tied the wings onto his arms. When he moved his arms the wings flapped.

"You *are* a bird," shouted Icarus. "Now make my wings quickly, Father."

Daedalus constructed a smaller set of wings for Icarus, and at last, early the next morning when everyone was asleep, father and son were ready to test them. "I shall go first," said Daedalus.

He spread his wings, flapped them, and up he rose, above the tower. He soared and glided up and down and around, while Icarus shouted, "Let me fly, too, Father! Let me fly!"

"Come," called Daedalus. "The wings work perfectly, and what a wonderful feeling it is to fly."

Icarus spread his wings, and he, too, soared and glided far above the tower, up into the sky. "Come back!" called Daedalus.

But Icarus did not return immediately. It was far too exciting to fly like a bird. When at last he came back, his father was angry. "You must do exactly as I say. We are not ready to leave yet. We must practice every morning until we are skillful enough to make our long trip to the mainland of Greece."

Early each morning, father and son practiced flying, with Icarus venturing farther and farther away, and Daedalus calling him back, speaking to him severely. "You must obey me, for flying is a tricky business. Tomorrow morning we shall set off on our flight of escape, and you must have your wits about you and follow my instructions."

"Oh, flying is easy," said Icarus. "I can even do it without looking."

"Never do that," said Daedalus. "You must steer carefully, taking a middle course. Not too low, near the sea, or your feathers will become damp and useless. And not too high, near the sun, or the wax that holds your feathers together will melt. Do you understand?"

"Of course!" said Icarus. But he was only half listening. He was much too excited about the journey, and, besides, he was tired of hearing his father's advice.

The next morning, Daedalus and Icarus put on their wings. Daedalus made sure that his son's wings were fastened on tightly. Then, his voice shaking, he said to Icarus, "Now we must be off.

Remember my advice, for you are very dear to me, and I fear for your safety."

They spread their wings, flapped them, and flew up into the air. Far below they saw farmers and shepherds looking up at them in astonishment.

They must think we are gods, thought Icarus, and he did a somersault in the air to show all the world that he was master of his wings. Then he followed his father, up and away, until he was flying over the expanse of blue sea.

Past the island of Delos they flew, on a middle course. But Icarus became impatient with following his father. He wanted to be on his own, flying anywhere he chose. First he swooped down toward the sea, flying as close to it as possible without dampening his feathers. Again and again he did it. It was like a game, and each time he was the winner.

I shall play the same game with the sun, he thought. He flew upward, higher and higher, nearer to the sun each time. *The wax does not melt*, he thought. *My father is too cautious.*

I shall fly just a little nearer, he thought, *until I am almost part of the sun. How powerful I shall feel then.*

He flapped his wings harder, until he was even closer to the sun. For an instant he felt radiant, like a god. Then, suddenly, he lost altitude. Down, down he fell, for the wax on his wings had melted with the sun's heat, and his feathers had come apart and scattered in every direction. He plunged into the sea.

When Daedalus looked back, Icarus was no longer following him. "Icarus!" he cried, over and over. "Where are you?" But there was no reply.

Daedalus flew frantically, searching the air, up and down. At last he spotted the feathers tossing about on the waves below, and he knew that his son was lost forever.

Daedalus buried Icarus on an island that he called Icaria, in memory of his son. Then he flew sadly to the island of Sicily, where he spent his remaining years.

Odysseus

THE TROJAN WAR

The long war between the Greeks and the Trojans began because of a quarrel among three goddesses. The quarrel came about in this way.

Eris, the goddess of discord, or disagreement, was angry. She had not been invited to the wedding of a king and a sea nymph, and so she decided to cause trouble. She threw a golden apple into the banquet hall. On it was written: *For the fairest*, and Aphrodite, Athena, and Hera each thought that the apple was hers.

Zeus knew that somebody must decide to whom the apple belonged, but he did not want to get into the argument. Instead he picked a handsome youth named Paris to act as judge. He said to the three goddesses, "Go to Mount Ida, where Paris, son of King Priam of Troy, is a shepherd. He will decide which of you is the fairest."

The three goddesses flew to Mount Ida, and each tried to bribe Paris to choose her. "I shall give you power and wealth," said Hera. "I shall give you glory and fame in battle," said Athena. "I shall give you the best gift of all," said Aphrodite. "The most beautiful woman in the world will be yours."

Paris had no difficulty in deciding. "The golden apple shall go to Aphrodite," he said. Then he turned to her and asked, "Oh, goddess of love, who *is* the most beautiful woman in the world?"

"Why, Helen, of course, the daughter of Zeus and Leda. Hundreds of suitors tried to win her, and now she is the happy wife of Menelaus, king of Sparta. But I shall make her fall in love with *you*!"

Aphrodite's son, Eros, shot an arrow of love into Helen's heart. She fell deeply in love with Paris and fled with him to Troy, far away on the eastern end of the Mediterranean Sea.

Helen's husband, Menelaus, called together Helen's past suitors and said, "We have all taken an oath to protect Helen. We must fight together to bring her home."

The men agreed, and soon they sailed to Troy with an army in a thousand ships. Among the soldiers was Odysseus, the king of Ithaca.

The city of Troy was well fortified by a strong, high wall. The Greeks and the Trojans fought countless battles outside the wall, but neither side could win. The bitter war went on for ten long years. It might have continued for many more, had not Odysseus thought up a clever plan.

"We have not been able to break down the strong wall of Troy by force," said Odysseus to the Greek soldiers. "Therefore we must trick the Trojans into opening the gates, so that our army can enter the city and destroy it."

First Odysseus directed the construction of an enormous, hollow wooden horse. It had a trapdoor on the underside, and an inscription dedicating it to the goddess Athena.

Next he instructed the Greeks to abandon their camp outside the wall of Troy. He told them to sail their ships away from the port and hide behind a nearby island. "The Trojans will think that our army has accepted defeat and gone home," he said. "But a group of our men will stay behind, hidden in the wooden horse. We will place the horse by the shore, outside the wall of Troy. And one man, Sinon, will stay behind in the camp to trick the Trojans into bringing the horse inside the gates."

Odysseus had the bravest Greek warriors climb up a rope ladder through the trapdoor and into the hollow horse. Menelaus, Helen's husband, was among them. Odysseus and his companions spent the long night waiting inside the wooden horse.

Early the next morning, one of the Trojan guards sighted something strange. "A huge wooden horse!" he shouted to the other guards. "Come quickly! Is it real, or is it my imagination?"

Just then a Trojan scout came running up, shouting, "The Greeks have abandoned their camp and sailed away."

The people of Troy heard their shouts and streamed out of the gates to the enemy camp. "It is true!" they cried. "The Greek army has gone. We have won the war!"

"But what is the meaning of this horse?" asked one.

"It is a gift meant for Athena," said another. "We must bring it into our city and take it to her temple."

"No! No!" cried Laocoön, a seer. "I fear Greeks, even when they bear gifts."

At that moment a group of Trojans dragged Sinon the Greek into their midst. Sinon told the tale that Odysseus had instructed him to tell: "The Greeks were going to kill me as a sacrifice to the goddess Athena, but I escaped. Now I wish to live as a Trojan."

The Trojans believed him, and they believed the rest of his story, too. "The huge wooden horse was made and left by the Greeks as an offering to Athena."

"But why did they make it so big?" asked a Trojan soldier.

"To discourage you Trojans from taking it into your city. They hope that you will destroy it and make Athena angry with you."

"Do not believe him," cried Laocoön. But just then, two huge serpents emerged from the sea and slithered toward Laocoön. They coiled themselves around him and squeezed him to death while the people watched helplessly.

"Laocoön has been punished by the gods," they cried. "The gods wish us to bring the wooden horse into our city and offer it to Athena."

"Yes! Yes!" cried the others. They acted quickly, dragging the heavy horse through the gates and up the hill to Athena's temple.

"Now," they said, "the war is over, and Athena will bless us with peace after ten years of terrible strife." They went to bed and slept soundly for the first time in all those years.

Inside the horse, Odysseus said to the men hidden there, "Our plan is working. All is quiet now. This is the moment we have been waiting for."

He opened the trapdoor, and he and the other Greek warriors climbed down the rope ladder. They crept to the gates of Troy and opened them. Then they signaled to the Greek army.

The Greeks marched into Troy and took the Trojans by surprise. In the terrible fighting that followed, most of the Trojan leaders lost their lives. At last the Greeks were victorious.

Aphrodite saved Helen and led her to her husband, Menelaus. They sailed for Greece, thankful that the long, bloody war was over.

THE VOYAGE OF ODYSSEUS

Finally Odysseus, too, set sail for home, anxious to see his wife, Penelope, and his son, Telemachus. But the gods were angry with the Greek warriors. After the victory at Troy, they had neglected to give thanks to the gods. And so Athena asked Poseidon to unloose a violent tempest to plague the homeward-bound Greek ships.

Poseidon's dreadful storm sank many of the ships. Although Odysseus's ships were spared, they were driven off course for nine wild, windy days. On the tenth day, Odysseus sighted land and sailed his ships into the harbor.

"We are safe at last," cried Odysseus. "We can rest here and take on a fresh supply of water. But first we must find out who lives in this land."

Odysseus sent three scouts to explore. But the scouts did not return, and Odysseus set off to look for them. When he found them, they were eating tiny, delicious fruit, and they had lost all memory of their task and of their homes, as well.

They offered some of the fruit to Odysseus, but instead of

taking it, he dashed the fruit from their hands. "This is the land of the lotus eaters," he said to his men. "Those who eat the fruit of the lotus plant lose all memory of home and long to stay in this land forever. You must come with me now, or you will never see your families again."

When the men refused to follow him, he dragged them to the ship and tied them securely, to keep them from returning.

Then they set sail for home.

*

After many days at sea, Odysseus again sighted land. Since he and the crews needed food and water, he beached his ships on the island. Little did he know that this was the land of the Cyclopes, ferocious giants with one huge eye in the middle of their foreheads. Once they had been metalsmiths and had forged thunderbolts for Zeus, but now they were shepherds and lived like wild animals in caves.

Odysseus and his men set off, carrying a goatskin full of wine as a gift to the inhabitants in return for supplies.

Soon they came to a large cave, and Odysseus entered first. "Come quickly!" he called. "The cave is filled with cheeses and bowls of milk."

They helped themselves to food and drink, not knowing that they were in the cave of Polyphemus, a son of Poseidon. He was one of the fiercest of the Cyclopes and particularly enjoyed eating humans.

Suddenly they heard the *clump-clump* of the giant's footsteps. Polyphemus entered the cave with his sheep and goats. He rolled an enormous rock into the cave's entrance to close it off. Then, looking down, he spotted Odysseus and his men.

"Who are you?" he bellowed in a voice like thunder. "What are you doing in my cave?"

"We are Greek warriors," said Odysseus, "bound for home after our victory at Troy. We seek your hospitality for the night."

The giant made no answer. Instead he grabbed two of the men, twirled them over his head, and flung them to the ground, killing them instantly. Then he made a meal of them and afterward lay down and fell asleep, snoring loudly.

Odysseus and the remaining men spent a terror-stricken night cowering in the corner of the cave. Odysseus could not kill the giant while he slept, for if he did, they would be trapped in the cave. Only the giant could roll aside the huge rock that sealed the entrance.

In the morning Polyphemus feasted on two more of Odysseus's men. Then he rolled away the rock and stomped out of the cave, driving his flocks before him. As he left, he rolled the rock back into place.

But now Odysseus had a plan. He hoisted a large stick of olive wood and sharpened it by turning it around in the fire. Then he and his men waited for Polyphemus to return.

That evening Polyphemus stomped into the cave again. He closed the entrance with the huge rock and started to milk his goats. Again he feasted on two of Odysseus's men. When he had finished, Odysseus offered him a large bowl of wine. The giant drank it in one gulp and asked for more. When Odysseus gave him another bowl, the giant thanked him and said, "Because of your gift of wine I shall do you a great favor."

"What is that?" said Odysseus, hoping to be freed.

"I shall eat you last," said the giant.

Then Polyphemus asked Odysseus his name, and Odysseus answered, "My name is Noman."

Finally the giant fell into a deep sleep brought on by the wine.

"This is the moment we have waited for," said Odysseus to his men. They sprang up, carrying the sharpened pole of wood, and heated it in the fire until it was red hot. Then they thrust the burning pole into the giant's one eye.

Polyphemus leaped up, screaming, "I have been blinded. Help! Help!" He hopped around the cave, bumping into the walls and knocking over the bowls of milk. Odysseus and his companions hid to avoid being trampled.

The Cyclopes who lived in the surrounding caves heard Polyphemus's screams and came running. "What has happened?" they called from outside the cave. But when Polyphemus replied that Noman had hurt him, they thought that all was well and went away.

Polyphemus groped for the rock that closed the entrance. He rolled it aside and blocked the opening with his huge body, shouting, "You rogues! You cannot escape from me, even though I am blind. I will catch you as you try to leave."

But Odysseus had planned for this moment, too. He and each of his men bound together three sheep. Then each man hung onto the underside of the middle sheep.

As the sheep passed out of the cave, Polyphemus felt them to make sure that the men were not riding them. But he did not think that the men would be *underneath* them. And so Odysseus and the surviving crew members escaped.

They drove the sheep onto their ships. And as they sailed away, Odysseus shouted, "O horrible Cyclops, if you want to know who it was that made you blind, it was I, Odysseus of Ithaca."

The giant hurled a rock at Odysseus's ship, trying to sink it. The rock fell into the water, just missing the ship.

Odysseus and his men rowed away, thankful for their escape.

But they did not know that the furious giant was praying to his father, Poseidon, to avenge him against his enemy, Odysseus.

And Poseidon heard the prayer and vowed revenge.

*

Odysseus sailed on toward home, thinking that his trials were over. He was unaware that more trouble awaited him.

Next he put in at the Island of the Winds. There lived King Aeolus, who governed the Four Winds, bidding them blow or be still. Aeolus was a generous host and saw to it that Odysseus and his men dined well. When they left, he gave Odysseus a leather bag tied tightly with a silver string.

"This bag holds all the dangerous storm winds," said King Aeolus. "If you keep it closed tightly, you will have no trouble on your journey. Now, remember, do not open the bag!"

Odysseus thanked King Aeolus and sailed confidently toward home with his fleet of ships. After he had been at the helm for nine days, he gave over command of his ship to one of his crew. Then he fell into a deep sleep.

This was the chance the crew had been waiting for. "Now we can open the bag," said one, "for surely it contains treasure. We can take some of it for ourselves."

They untied the string and out rushed the dangerous winds, causing a violent tempest. The ships were driven far off course and finally back to the Island of the Winds. King Aeolus was so angry that he refused to help them again, and Odysseus and his men were forced to row away.

*

After many days, all the ships except the one carrying Odysseus entered a harbor that seemed secure and anchored there. From his position outside the harbor, Odysseus witnessed a terrible scene. The savage inhabitants of the land were attacking the ships. They sank them all and killed the men. Odysseus and his crew rowed away with all their might. Only they survived, sick at heart over the fate of their comrades.

*

Circe the sorceress ruled over the island on which Odysseus next landed. It looked a pleasant place, filled with large shady trees, and on the top of a hill stood a sumptuous palace. Odysseus sent a group of his men to explore the island and seek hospitality.

As the men neared the palace, they were surrounded by wolves and lions and tigers. But the animals were tame and did not attack them. That was because they were really men. Circe's magic had made them look like beasts.

Odysseus's men did not know that Circe was a witch and could work such evil magic. They hurried up the hill to the palace, enticed by a sweet female voice singing a soft melody.

Circe greeted them at the door and lured them inside with a smile. "Come and dine with me," she crooned in a honeyed voice.

The men accepted gladly, bolting down the cheeses and fruits and meats, a feast such as they had dreamed of on their long voyage. Only Eurylochus, one of the crew, remained outside, for he was suspicious. He watched through the window as the men became sleepy from the drugged food and wine. Then he saw Circe touch each man with her wand and turn them, one by one, into pigs.

Circe herded the pigs into a pen, threw them acorns to eat, and shut the gate tightly.

Eurylochus ran back to the ship and cried to Odysseus, "The men have been changed into pigs by a wicked sorceress. What shall we do?"

Odysseus said, "I shall go there alone and rescue them."

He walked slowly, trying to think of a way to outwit Circe. But no plan came to him. On the way he met a youth who

introduced himself as the god Hermes. Hermes warned him that Circe was a dangerous witch, and he gave Odysseus a magic flower. "This flower," he said, "will protect you from Circe's magic."

Odysseus thanked him and strode up the hill to Circe's palace, clutching the flower. After he had eaten her drugged feast, she touched him with her wand, saying, "Now you shall become a pig and join your comrades in the pen."

But Odysseus's magic flower saved him. He rushed at Circe with drawn sword, and she knelt at his feet, crying, "Have mercy on me! Please spare me!"

"I shall spare you only if you agree to turn my comrades back into men and set them free. And you must swear that you will not harm us in any way."

Circe took an oath, promising to help Odysseus and his men. She released them from the magic spell, and afterward she entertained Odysseus and his crew for a whole year. They accepted her hospitality gratefully, eating and drinking their fill, listening to her soft music, and resting on silken sheets.

*

At last, having had enough of ease and plenty, they were ready to set sail for home.

Circe agreed to let them leave, but she told Odysseus that before resuming his homeward voyage he must visit the underworld alone. "There you must seek the advice of a seer named

Teiresias," she said. "He will tell you the fate that awaits you on the rest of your journey."

Then she gave Odysseus detailed instructions on how to reach the underworld and how to make the seer come to him.

When he arrived in the underworld, Odysseus followed Circe's advice. He dug a trench, killed two sheep, and let their blood flow into the trench. While he waited for the ghost of Teiresias to come and drink the blood, he had to fight off other ghosts, for all the spirits thirsted for blood.

At last the ghost of Teiresias appeared, drank his fill of blood, and answered Odysseus's question: "What must I do to reach home safely?"

"You must not let your men harm the cattle of Helios, the sun. Doom awaits anyone who injures one of those prized cattle."

"I will warn my men when that times comes," said Odysseus.

The seer also told Odysseus that he would reach home but would find many enemies there. "Do not despair, however, for you shall overcome them."

The throng of ghosts pressed around Odysseus as he thanked the seer. They drank the remaining blood greedily and then spoke to Odysseus. Among them were ghosts of royalty and of warriors from the Trojan War, some of whom had been his friends. Though Odysseus was glad to speak to them, he was gladder still to make his escape and rejoin his men on shipboard.

*

Circe had also sent Odysseus on his way with a warning: "Beware of the sea nymphs called Sirens. They entice sailors with their sweet songs, promising them their heart's desire and causing them to jump into the sea and be lost forever." Circe had advised Odysseus how to withstand them, and when his ship passed the Island of the Sirens, he followed her instructions.

He said to his crew, "Put this wax in your ears. Then you will be deaf to the Sirens' songs and will avoid flinging yourselves into the sea."

Odysseus, however, did not plug his own ears with wax, for he was curious about these songs. He wanted to hear them, to know their mysteries. He commanded his crew, "Tie me to the mast as we sail past, and by no means release me, no matter how I plead with you."

His men did as they were told, and as Odysseus heard the Sirens' songs, he strained to break his bonds and follow the notes into the sea. So great was his longing that he shouted to his crew, "Untie me, I beg of you. I must swim to the Sirens. Their songs promise that I shall know the future. Untie me this instant!"

But the crew kept him tied until the notes became fainter and fainter, and finally Odysseus could hear them no more. Only when they were safely past did the crew release him.

*

Next Odysseus had to sail his ship through the narrow strait guarded by the sea monsters Scylla and Charybdis.

Odysseus kept careful watch and steered his ship skillfully around Charybdis's churning waters. But he sailed too near the other monster. Scylla, with her six heads, darted out from her cave in the opposite cliff. She snatched one crew member with each mouth and devoured them with a terrible crunching noise while Odysseus and the crew watched, horrified. Odysseus and the others sailed away, thankful for their escape.

*

Then Odysseus sailed to the Island of the Sun. As the ship landed, he warned his crew, "I have heard that the cattle of Helios, the sun, are pastured here. But no matter how hungry you are, you must not eat a single animal. Remember the warning of the seer in the underworld."

The crew swore that they would not so much as touch the cattle. However, due to unfavorable winds, Odysseus and his men were stranded on the island for a month, and their food supply ran out.

At last Eurylochus said to a group of the men, "We have fished and hunted for food, but without luck. We have no choice but to kill the cattle."

The men agreed, and when Odysseus was asleep, they butchered several of the cattle, roasted them, and had a fine meal.

Helios was furious. He insisted that Zeus punish Odysseus's men. Zeus, also angry, hurled a thunderbolt, which destroyed Odysseus's ship and drowned all but Odysseus.

*

Resourceful Odysseus made a raft by lashing together part of the mast and keel. Many days later he drifted to an island. It was ruled by a sea nymph named Calypso.

Odysseus spent years shipwrecked on Calypso's island, for she loved him and would not let him leave. Finally Zeus took pity on him and commanded Calypso to help Odysseus build a raft and supply him with provisions. And at last he steered for Ithaca, thinking, *Soon I shall see my wife and son.*

But Poseidon sent a gigantic wave to sweep Odysseus into the sea. Odysseus was a strong swimmer. Still, he might not have survived without the help of Ino, a sea nymph who appeared in the form of a seagull. She gave him a present, a belt that kept him afloat until finally he drifted ashore.

*

Odysseus had arrived at an island ruled by King Alcinoüs. He fell asleep there, beside a stream.

The next morning he was awakened by the cry of a lovely maiden. "Oh, dear, now we can't finish our game," she called to her friends. "Our ball has landed in the stream."

She ran to the stream and watched as the ball was carried

away. But she soon forgot about the ball, for she was startled at the sudden appearance of a disheveled man clad only in leaves.

Her fears vanished when Odysseus told her who he was and asked for her help. She introduced herself as Nausicaä, daughter of the king, and arranged for him to see her father.

When King Alcinoüs heard the long tale of Odysseus's adventures, he gave him many gifts and a sturdy ship in which to sail home.

*

At last, ten years after the start of his voyage, Odysseus reached Ithaca. He had been gone for twenty years in all, and he did not even recognize his own land. But Athena, disguised as a shepherd, appeared to him and told him that he was home.

"Home!" cried Odysseus. "Is it really possible?"

"Yes," said Athena, "but your troubles are not over. One hundred twelve suitors are vying for the hand of your wife, Penelope. They hope to take your place as king.

"Penelope resisted these suitors for many years," Athena continued. "She told them that she would choose one only after she had finished weaving a shroud for your father. For three years, she wove by day and unraveled the shroud by night. But the suitors finally found her out, and now, certain that you are dead, she has proclaimed that the winner of an archery contest will win her hand in marriage."

Athena turned Odysseus into an old beggar so that he would

not be recognized by his enemies, the suitors. Then, with the help of Athena and his fine grown son, Telemachus, Odysseus won the contest and slew Penelope's suitors.

Finally Odysseus revealed himself to his wife, and they were reunited at last. And, after twenty years, he regained his throne. A great banquet was held to celebrate the joyous homecoming.

The Constellations

Orion

ORION was a giant and a brave hunter. He could walk on water, a gift given him by his father, Poseidon, god of the sea.

One day Orion walked across the water to the island of Chios. There he fell in love with the king's daughter, Merope.

Orion said to the king, "I wish to marry your daughter, for I have fallen deeply in love with her. Tell me what I must do to gain her hand."

"Very well," said the king. "Since you are famous as a mighty hunter, you must rid my island of lions and bears and wolves. Only then will I give you my precious daughter's hand in marriage."

Orion strode through the hills and killed all the wild animals with his sword and his club. Then he brought their skins to the king and said, "Now I have finished my task. Let us set a day for the wedding."

But the king did not want to part with his daughter and

kept putting off the wedding date. This angered Orion, and he tried to carry off Merope.

Her father retaliated. He called on the god of wine, Dionysus, to put Orion into a drunken sleep. Then the king blinded Orion and flung him onto the sand by the sea.

When Orion awoke sightless, he cried out, "I am blind and helpless. How shall I ever hunt again or win Merope for my bride?"

In his despair, Orion consulted an oracle, which answered him, "O Orion, you shall regain your sight if you travel east to the place where the sun rises. The warm rays of the sun shall heal your eyes and restore their power."

But how could a blind man find his way to that distant

place? Orion followed the sound of the Cyclopes' hammers to the forge of the god Hephaestus. When the god saw the blind hunter, he took pity on him and gave him a guide to lead him to the sun, just as it was rising.

Orion raised his eyes to the sun and, miraculously, he could see again. After thanking the sun, Orion set off for the island of Chios to take revenge on the king. But the king and his daughter had fled, possibly to Crete, and Orion went there to look for them. He never found them, but he met up with Artemis, goddess of the hunt, and spent his days hunting with her. They were a happy pair, roving through the woods, until Artemis's brother, Apollo, became jealous.

Apollo sent a scorpion to attack Orion. Orion could not pierce the scorpion's tough body with his arrows, but he dodged the poisonous insect and strode far out to sea.

Apollo was bent on destroying Orion, and he called to Artemis, "See that rock way out there in the sea? I challenge you to hit it."

Artemis loved a challenge. She drew her bow and aimed carefully. Her first arrow hit the mark, and Apollo congratulated her on her skill.

But when the waves brought Orion's body to the shore, Artemis moaned with grief. "I have killed my beloved companion. I shall never forget him. And the world shall never forget him, either."

She lifted his body up into the sky, where he remains among the stars to this day—the mighty hunter, one of the most brilliant constellations, with his sword and his club and three bright stars for his belt.

Cassiopeia

Cassiopeia, wife of King Cepheus of Ethiopia, boasted to the sea nymphs, "I and my daughter, Andromeda, are far more beautiful than you. You are plain next to us."

The lovely sea nymphs swam to Poseidon, god of the sea, to tell him about Cassiopeia's insult. "You must punish Cassiopeia," they said. "She must not get away with such boasting."

Poseidon acted quickly. He sent a huge and hungry sea

monster to Ethiopia to devour scores of King Cepheus's people.

King Cepheus was distraught, and he asked an oracle, "What must I do to rid my country of this ferocious monster?"

The oracle replied, "Chain your daughter, Andromeda, to a rock by the sea. Leave her there for the sea monster to feast upon. Only in this way shall you be rid of it."

To his wife's despair, King Cephcus did as he was told, and poor Andromeda awaited her fate, chained and helpless. But as the sea monster was about to devour her, the hero Perseus flew overhead in Hermes' winged sandals. Just in time, he landed on the monster's back and thrust his sword into it repeatedly. After a raging battle, Perseus killed the monster and carried away the lovely Andromeda, who became his bride.

Perseus and Andromeda lived happily together, but the sea nymphs never forgot Cassiopeia's insult. Many years later, when Cassiopeia died, the sea nymphs again begged Poseidon to punish her.

This time Poseidon did so by setting Cassiopeia in the north sky in a most uncomfortable position. She sits in a high-backed chair that looks like a *W*—but during part of the year, the chair hangs upside down.

Near Cassiopeia, Athena placed the constellation Andromeda, and Andromeda's brave husband, Perseus, stands not far from her in the Milky Way. Cepheus is there, too, though dimmer, and so is Cetus, the sea monster, also called the Whale.

Castor and Pollux

Castor and Pollux were inseparable twin brothers. Their father was Zeus, and their mother was a mortal, Leda of Sparta.

They were strong, athletic young men. Castor was renowned as a soldier and tamer of horses, and Pollux was an outstanding boxer. Both entered the Olympic games and won many competitions. They were worshipped as gods by athletes, soldiers, and sailors.

Castor and Pollux were among the Argonauts, who aided Jason in his quest for the Golden Fleece. But after their return, they had a dispute with two young men. A terrible battle followed, and Castor, who was mortal, was killed. Pollux, who was immortal, wept over the body of his twin. He cried to his father, Zeus, "Please let me kill myself and follow my brother to the underworld. I feel that half of myself is gone, and the half that remains is but a shadow."

Zeus took pity on Pollux and said, "Though I cannot enable you to die, for you are immortal, I shall allow you and Castor to be together always. Together you shall spend alternate days

in the underworld and on Olympus. And because of your great love for your brother, I shall raise your images into the sky. There you shall shine next to each other forever."

And Castor and Pollux became the twin stars, forming the constellation Gemini.

Afterword

The best stories about ancient Greek gods and heroes concern the Trojan War, the ten-year war fought by Greece against the city of Troy. These tales of the Trojan War, contained in the ancient Greek poems of the *Iliad* and the *Odyssey*, are combinations of myths and legends.

Myths are stories about divine beings and nature. They tell us how the Greeks understood the world before science, as we know it, existed. Because of what science teaches us, and because we do not believe that Zeus or Hera or any of the other gods really existed, we do not accept myths as fact.

Legends, however, are at least based on history. For example, we know that there really was a Troy, a city in what we call northwest Turkey, and that it was destroyed about 1200 B.C. It was not a powerful city and there was not a big war, but some little seed of fact did grow into the flourishing plant of Greek stories about Troy. One of these stories concerns the hero Odysseus, his adventures on the ten-year trip home from the war, and how he dealt with the situation he found back home.

Odysseus and the others who had attacked Troy were Greeks. What about the Trojans? The Trojan hero Aeneas, son of the goddess Aphrodite, reportedly survived the fall of Troy and escaped with other Trojans to Italy. The Romans, an ancient Italian people, told this tale in the third great epic poem, the *Aeneid*.

Basically, this story was an attempt by the Romans, who became political rulers of the Greeks, to connect themselves to Greek mythology. Another way the Romans did this was by associating a native Italian god or goddess with a Greek one who had similar traits and powers. The following list presents the Roman names for Greek deities:

GREEK NAME	ROMAN NAME
Zeus	Jupiter
Poseidon	Neptune
Hades or Pluto	Dis or Orcus
Hera	Juno
Athena or Pallas	Minerva
Aphrodite	Venus
Hestia	Vesta
Ares	Mars
Apollo	Apollo
Artemis	Diana
Demeter	Ceres
Hephaestus	Vulcan
Hermes	Mercury

These gods were not exactly alike. The Greek god of war, Ares, was a stupid bully, while the Roman god of war, Mars, was a highly respected deity. This difference reflects the different attitude of most Greeks and Romans toward war. Since the Romans did not have a native god with the qualities of the Greek Apollo—concern for truth, music, healing, and light—they simply borrowed Apollo himself. This, too, shows the different values of the early Greek and Roman civilizations.

Greek mythology, as you now know, is immensely entertaining. It is also a mine of information about the history, the understanding of nature, and the values of the mythmakers. And it is thanks not only to the Greeks—who created them—but also to the Romans—who preserved and added to them—that we will always have this treasure.

Index